Praise for
Miracle on Hope Hill

"If you like to be surprised by joy, then read *Miracle on Hope Hill*. The timeless stories in this treasured book will remind you that even when life doesn't make sense, hope keeps shining like a bright candle in the dark night. You'll read it, love it, and read it again!"
—Alice Gray, author of the bestselling *Stories for the Heart* collection and coauthor of *The Worn Out Woman*

"A good story, like a wise proverb, is priceless. When family, friends, or congregations can share together the kind of true stories that Carol and Jennie tell in *Miracle on Hope Hill*, they have found a way of saying together that, even in our darkest moments, there is hope."
—Martin De Haan, president of RBC Ministries, international publisher of *Our Daily Bread*

"*Miracle on Hope Hill* is the perfect, uplifting read when life feels challenging—whether you're personally struggling or feeling the weight of the world's traumas and tragedies. Through the stories that Carol and Jennie share, you'll remember that God is faithful and present through it all, even the hard stuff, and often working behind the scenes . . . or, sometimes, taking front and center stage!"
—Lisa T. Bergren, author of *The Busy Mom's Devotional* and coauthor of *What Women Want*

"Lovingly reminding us there are no accidents in God's grand plan, Carol and Jennie present a refreshing and powerful reminder that God is indeed in control and he loves us beyond comprehension. An uplifting collection of God's love in action, the stories in *Miracle on Hope Hill* are filled with spiritual insight and inspiring truth."
—Allison Bottke, author of *Setting Boundaries with Your Adult Children*; founder, God Allows U-Turns

"Fewer things are more powerful than real-life stories that inspire and move our lives toward greater good. A big thanks to Carol and Jennie for harvesting and compiling these transformational stories!"

—Joseph M. Stowell, president, Cornerstone University

"The dynamic duo of Carol Kent and Jennie Afman Dimkoff have combined to masterfully communicate encouraging stories that illustrate God's personal involvement and love in the everyday details of our lives. As you read, you'll be reminded of God's faithfulness in both little and big ways—from a desire for the right dress to life-threatening needs. Heart-lifting reminders of God in action, working to do far beyond all that we can ask or dream!"

—LeAnn Weiss-Rupard, coauthor of *Hugs* and founder of Encouragement Company

"Whether God sneaks in like a church mouse or moves like a lightning bolt, when he shows up, at just the right time, you know it! Thank you, Carol Kent and Jennie Dimkoff, for bringing us real-life stories of God's goodness, greatness, and power. With each story, faith is strengthened, loads lifted, and spirits renewed. After reading this book, readers will be more aware that God is on active duty in their lives!"

—Chrys Howard, bestselling author of *Motivationals for Moms*

MIRACLE

on

HOPE HILL

AND OTHER TRUE STORIES
OF GOD'S LOVE

CAROL KENT
and
JENNIE AFMAN DIMKOFF

HOWARD BOOKS
A DIVISION OF SIMON & SCHUSTER, INC.

NEW YORK   NASHVILLE   LONDON   TORONTO   SYDNEY   NEW DELHI

Published by Howard Books, a division of Simon & Schuster, Inc.
1230 Avenue of the Americas, New York, NY 10020

Copyright © 2011 by Carol Kent and Jennie Afman Dimkoff

Scripture quotations marked NIV are taken from the Holy Bible, New International Version®, NIV®. Copyright © 1973, 1978, 1984 by Biblica, Inc.™ Used by permission of Zondervan. All rights reserved worldwide. www.zondervan.com. Scripture quotations marked MSG are taken from The Message. Copyright © 1993, 1994, 1995, 1996, 2000, 2001, 2002. Used by permission of NavPress Publishing Group. Scripture quotations marked NLT are taken from the Holy Bible, New Living Translation, copyright 1996, 2004, 2007 by Tyndale House Foundation. Used by permission of Tyndale House Publishers, Inc., Carol Stream, Illinois 60188. All rights reserved. Scripture quotations marked TLB are taken from The Living Bible copyright © 1971. Used by permission of Tyndale House Publishers, Inc., Wheaton, IL 60189. All rights reserved. Scripture quotations marked NCV are quoted from The Holy Bible, New Century Version, copyright © 1987, 1988, 1991 by Word Publishing, Nashville, Tennessee. Used by permission. Scripture quotations marked NKJV are taken from the New King James Version. Copyright © 1982 by Thomas Nelson, Inc. Used by permission. All rights reserved. Scripture quotations marked KJV are taken from the King James Version of the Bible. Public domain. Scripture quotations marked ESV are from The Holy Bible, English Standard Version, copyright © 2001 by Crossway Bibles, a division of Good News Publishers. Used by permission. All rights reserved. Scripture quotations marked NASB are taken from the New American Standard Bible®, Copyright © 1960, 1962, 1963, 1968, 1971, 1972, 1973, 1975, 1977, 1995 by The Lockman Foundation. Used by permission.

Some of the names throughout this book have been changed to protect the privacy of the people involved.

First Howard Books hardcover edition October 2011

HOWARD and colophon are trademarks of Simon & Schuster, Inc.

For information about special discounts for bulk purchases, please contact Simon & Schuster Special Sales at 1-866-506-1949 or business@simonandschuster.com.

The Simon & Schuster Speakers Bureau can bring authors to your live event. For more information or to book an event contact the Simon & Schuster Speakers Bureau at 1-866-248-3049 or visit our website at www.simonspeakers.com.

Designed by Kyoko Watanabe

Manufactured in the United States of America

10   9   8   7   6   5   4   3   2   1

Library of Congress Cataloging-in-Publication Data
Kent, Carol, 1947–
Miracle on Hope Hill : and other true stories of God's love / Carol Kent and Jennie Afman Dimkoff.
p. cm.
Includes bibliographical references.
1. God (Christianity)—Love—Anecdotes. 2. Miracles—Anecdotes.
I. Dimkoff, Jennie Afman. II. Title.
BT140.K48 2011
231.7'3—dc22   2011003810

ISBN 978-1-5011-2921-6

To my husband,
Gene Kent.

Thank you for being my lifelong partner,
my source of stability and courage, and for providing
a great balance of humor and hope in each day.
I love "doing life" with you!

Carol

To my husband,
Graydon W. Dimkoff.

Thanks for all the years of loving, dreaming,
providing, parenting, goal planning, praying, and playing.
Honey, thank you for encouraging me to write—
and for never losing that twinkle in your eyes.

Love always, Jennie

CONTENTS

MIRACLE
on
HOPE HILL

> A stranger is just a friend I haven't met yet.[1]
> —WILL ROGERS

CHAPTER 1

Unexpected Company

BY CAROL KENT

"Never pick up a stranger! Don't take candy from someone you don't know." The adults in Vicky's life during her growing-up years were very clear: "Strangers are scary—avoid them!"

But those early warnings lessened in Vicky's mind after Hurricane Katrina ravaged the Gulf Coast. A week after that massive storm hit New Orleans, she received a call from her college friend Dianne. Dianne had evacuated and was staying with relatives out of state. Vicky, who lived in Baton Rouge, had tried to reach her friend several times, but cell phone service was intermittent at best and most often nonexistent.

Once they connected, Dianne asked if Vicky knew of any rental properties in the Baton Rouge area, which was only an hour's drive from her flooded home. She explained that she needed a furnished place since, by all reports, she had lost everything. Vicky knew there was nothing available—no vacant houses, no apartments, and the hotels were already full. Her response was speedy. "Just come to my house. I'd be glad to take you in."

Dianne had been running a transitional home for women who were trying to get off the streets, off drugs, or both. Vicky had a suspicion that Dianne had not evacuated alone. The words tumbled off her tongue. "Please, feel free to bring whoever is with you."

They came, and for the next several months Vicky housed

and fed her friend, along with two additional women Dianne brought with her. One came with a history of cocaine addiction. The other had a background in prostitution. In Vicky's pre-Katrina life, she'd never met a prostitute and had never laid eyes on cocaine, so everything about this experience was brand-new. One day she smiled, thinking, *It isn't that I hate adventure; I just prefer roller coasters where someone makes sure I'm safely strapped in. This entire Katrina thing is different from anything I've ever experienced.*

What followed next was even more unexpected. Dianne's elderly neighbor Muriel had not evacuated, in spite of Dianne's insistence that she leave. Dianne grieved, presuming her neighbor had died. Muriel was eighty-five years old and spent most of her day in a power wheelchair due to post-polio syndrome. It would have been a miracle for her to escape the rising waters.

• • •

Muriel's story was harrowing. She was fine when the hurricane hit the mainland, but she was in deep trouble when water began quickly and forcefully flooding into her home. Her mind raced: *I know as soon as the water reaches the wheelchair batteries, I'll be stranded.* She moved to the side of her bed as quickly as possible. Due to Muriel's physical disability, she usually did a front transfer of her body to her bed, not a side transfer. She needed to get onto her bed, set up her manual chair, and transfer into it from the bed.

Her thoughts swirled as she realized there was not enough time for her to set up the manual chair, position herself in it, and get to her front door in time to unlock the dead bolt. The water was rising quickly. Working as fast as she could, she set up the manual chair while she was still seated in the power chair. Later, she explained what happened next. "I felt a presence, Vicky. Someone picked me up and put me in the other chair. Even though I was alone, arms encircled me and lifted me out of one chair and into the next."

Muriel didn't have time to ponder the miracle of what had just happened. She quickly wheeled herself through the rising waters to the front of the house, and at that moment she heard someone banging on her door. Neighbors presumed she might still be in her home and were checking on her. By the time Muriel got the door open, they had gone back down her front steps, and several men were in the street with water up to their chests.

Muriel called out, and the men returned. Before knocking on Muriel's door, they had made their way down the street to a home where they knew the owner kept a boat. Once it was secured, they lifted Muriel into the boat—but they discovered the boat had a hole in the side. Two of the men pulled the boat through the water. One man bailed out the incoming water with a plastic bucket, and another sat behind Muriel in the boat to steady her.

Navigating down the flooded street, they eventually arrived at their destination—a two-story house. The men carefully carried Muriel up a narrow staircase to a bedroom that was already filled with at least twelve other people. Assured of her temporary safety, the men returned to Muriel's home, recovered her small fold-up wheelchair, and brought it to her new location.

After spending one night in the hot, stuffy upstairs room, a Coast Guard boat arrived. Men inside the house carried Muriel out through a window onto the sloping roof of the first-story porch. Carefully, her rescuers lowered Muriel from the roof into another boat. Later, Muriel commented, "How these men were able to get me to safety is a feat I still don't understand. Even though I had experienced the miracle transfer from my power wheelchair to my manual chair, I seriously doubted I would survive."

• • •

Vicky arrived home from work, and Dianne enthusiastically reported, "You will never believe who called me today—Muriel! She's alive and she's in Houston!" She asked Vicky if her Bible study girlfriends would consider adopting Muriel. The women began sending little packages and cards to this woman they had never met—a stranger who needed help. Vicky later said, "An almost instant bond was created between us."

Vicky had multiple conversations with Muriel about what her next step would be. Vicky and Dianne were able to make arrangements for her to get a FEMA trailer in New Orleans, but they knew that was just one more temporary solution. Muriel longed to be back in her home, to feel settled again in a familiar place. As time passed, Muriel realized her neighborhood was never going to be the same. It became apparent that the task of repairing her home to make it habitable again was too great an undertaking for someone her age and too great a burden for her limited resources. She commented, "If I were fifty years younger, I would do it."

During this time, Vicky's friend Alicia spoke up. "Muriel just needs to come and live with *you*." Vicky was single and had a four-bedroom house, but this was *not* an ideal solution for multiple reasons. Muriel's wheelchair was too wide for the two bathroom doors in Vicky's home, and her entire home was not wheelchair friendly. Besides, Dianne and the other two women from New Orleans had already relocated, so Vicky's life was just becoming "normal" again.

Vicky turned to Alicia and said, "No, no, no, keep thinking of another solution."

One day, as Vicky backed out of her driveway, her eyes

locked on the storage and workshop area that was connected to the back of her home. Her body froze, but her mind was racing. *What if that area was gutted and transformed into a wheelchair-accessible suite for Muriel?*

Vicky instantly realized this was not a plan she would have come up with on her own, and she called Muriel. "I have an idea. You could come and live with me." Vicky explained the idea of remodeling her workshop to accommodate Muriel's wheelchair and waited for a response.

Muriel's heart had already been moved by the tangible love and compassion of Vicky and her friends, and she immediately said, "I can't think of anyplace I would rather be."

The plan was in motion—until Vicky got the quotes on the cost of doing the remodeling job. The workshop area had electricity, but there was no plumbing. It needed new interior walls, a roll-in shower, and cabinets. The cost was overwhelming, and neither Muriel nor Vicky had the necessary funds.

Word was starting to spread about the unique connection Vicky had with a victim of Hurricane Katrina, and Mac, a retired man in her church, approached her after Sunday services the following weekend. "Can I come and look at what you're wanting to do?" he asked cheerfully. "I think I might be able to do some of the work."

Clayton, another man from the church, said, "You've bitten off more than you can chew here. I'll work on organizing some volunteers."

What happened during the next few months was nothing short of a miracle. Jack, the contractor, provided his services for free. Mac showed up during the week to work, and Clayton and his volunteers were there every Saturday. Jerry, another volunteer, bought a side-by-side refrigerator for the suite so Muriel would have access from her wheelchair. Jack inspected the volunteers' work and met with Clayton during the week to go over what needed to happen next. Women showed up to paint. They made curtains and shopped for bedding.

Young men in the college ministry volunteered to dig the water and sewer lines. On the morning the sewer line was to be dug, Vicky was anxious, knowing there wasn't enough help for this massive job. Then she gazed out the window and watched two vehicles pull up. The doors opened, and five Louisiana State University students filed out and pulled out their shovels. The job was finished in record time. With the extraordinary help of countless individuals, Muriel's suite was built, and the woman who had once been a stranger became family.

Therefore welcome one another as Christ has welcomed you, for the glory of God.

—ROMANS 15:7 ESV

> The greatest thing a man can do for a Heavenly Father . . . is to be kind to some of His other children.[1]
> —HENRY DRUMMOND

CHAPTER 2

The Secret Marriage

BY JENNIE AFMAN DIMKOFF

"Ma'am, would you know of a room for rent in this neighborhood?"

Ella dried her wet hands on a towel as she studied the young man through her screen door.

"I have employment, ma'am, but I need a room to rent," added the handsome soldier, standing on her doorstep wearing an army uniform, his duffel bag at his feet.

The year was 1946, and Ella and John had two little daughters and *no* intention of renting their extra bedroom out to anyone. However, something tugged at Ella's heart. Her brother had died in the war, and the young man standing there in his uniform reminded her so much of him that she couldn't turn him away.

"Well . . . I'm not sure. Wait here a moment, all right?"

Ella rushed off to find her husband, and a few minutes later, Clyde Afman was welcomed into their home.

"We have a few rules," the homeowners explained to their new tenant, and they made it clear that their extra room would only be available to *one* person. No buddies should plan on bunking with him.

That night Clyde climbed into bed and marveled at God's goodness. He had completed his tour of duty and returned from Germany unscathed when so many hadn't. His new job was secure, and now God had provided this room with a wonderful family at a cost he could afford. He shook his head in wonder. It had been the very first door he had dared to knock on! And the house was not only close to work, but it was also only seventeen miles away from Pauline! He fell asleep with a smile on his face, remembering the night he met her for the first time.

• • •

Twenty-two years old and single, Pauline and her girlfriend were having fun. A conservative minister's daughter, Pauline worked at the Kent County treasurer's office and also part-time as a switchboard operator. She loved to go to the roller rink and forget the sadness of war. She had dated a lot during those years, had been engaged several times, and had her heart broken, but that Monday night she just wanted to have fun.

She noticed the tall, handsome, uniformed soldier by the time she circled the floor twice. When he passed her the first time and caught her eye and smiled, her heart skipped a beat, and she smiled right back. The next time around, he held out his hand.

"Care to skate with me?"

When Pauline nodded, the megawatt smile she gave him almost made Clyde stumble! Song after song they skated together, and when the evening was over, he asked to see her home, where they had cake and milk and talked for hours. She already had a date for the following night, so they agreed to meet on Wednesday evening. He arrived early. As the week went by, they saw each other nightly, learning more and more about one another. Pauline was thrilled to learn that Clyde was a Christian and not afraid to speak of spiritual things. As their time together drew to a close, every moment was precious and young love began to blossom.

Clyde Afman had never felt like this about anyone before.

However, there was one important secret he hadn't told Pauline. He was already engaged to someone else! Before he left to take the train back to his base in California, he confessed that he was pledged to another woman but that he would end that relationship. He gave Pauline one chaste kiss and was gone.

Back in California, Clyde took his first available furlough and hitchhiked all the way to Texas to humbly seek the forgiveness of the woman he had proposed to earlier and to tell her face-to-face that he had met someone else. It was a difficult trip physically and emotionally but once completed, he was a free man.

Writing to Pauline, he told her what he had done, and their correspondence began. He completed his military commitment in California and was finally free to go back and profess his love to the woman he longed to marry, hitchhiking all the way from California to Michigan. He proposed the first night he saw her . . . and then every night for a week before she said yes.

Now that he was working and living just seventeen miles from Pauline, Clyde rode the city bus into Grand Rapids multiple times a week so that they could be together. He loved being with her, but he got no welcome from Pauline's brothers and that bothered him. Her mother had passed away three years before, and her father was a formidable minister who wasn't pleased that his daughter had chosen someone from outside their conservative denomination to marry. However, he was willing to perform the ceremony.

As weeks and months passed, a wedding date was set, but instead of joy, Pauline felt only tension. She desperately wanted to marry Clyde, and yet, she was anguished over the disapproval of her family. When her girlfriend eloped and got married with only a blood test and no waiting period, an idea took root.

"Couldn't we do the same thing—run away and get married?" Pauline asked Clyde. "It would be official, and then no one could talk us out of it!"

They decided that they would elope and just continue to live separate lives, not telling anyone they were really married until after the wedding date they had originally set. That way, they wouldn't hurt her father's feelings or risk the wrath of her brothers.

And so they did. The excitement lasted for a day or two until the secret, and their longing to be together as man and wife, started taking its toll. They kept their marriage a secret for a month until they finally couldn't take it any longer. Clyde came into town on the bus and found Pauline close to tears.

"I just can't stand the deception anymore, Clyde. I want us to tell them. Let's tell them tonight!" Pauline was weeping now.

"Are you sure, honey? Don't cry. Don't you want your father to perform your wedding ceremony?"

"I want to be with you, and I can't stand living a lie! I'm going crazy with you just coming to visit me. We have to tell them tonight!"

And so, a family meeting was called with her father and four siblings in attendance. It did not go well.

Afterward, while Clyde waited on the porch, his tearful bride went up to her bedroom; stuffed a nightgown, her toothbrush, some underclothes, and a few other items inside her pillowcase; and came back downstairs. Clyde placed his arm around his distraught bride, who was clinging to the pillowcase as if her life depended on it. Knowing that the eyes of his in-laws were watching from the windows, he led Pauline toward the bus stop. They faced several serious obstacles. The first was that they were seventeen miles from his room in Cutlerville, and the last bus left at nine PM. It was already nine thirty. Facing the traffic, he stuck out his thumb.

An elderly couple driving a Model A Ford came upon an unusual sight. There on the side of the road was a forlorn young couple. The young man was hitchhiking, and the young woman, who was clinging to his arm with one hand and to an overstuffed pillow with the other, had obviously been weeping.

"Where are you young folks headed?" the old fellow asked.

Sighing with relief, Clyde answered, "Cutlerville, sir." Turning, he gave Pauline a kiss on the cheek and added, "We're on our honeymoon."

"Well, whaddaya know?" The old man grinned. "Me and the missus are headed to Cutlerville! We'll take you right to your door. Honeymooners, eh? Did you hear that, Hazel?"

The ride for the entire seventeen miles was a gift indeed, but the closer they got, the heavier Clyde's heart became. Ella and John had been so gracious about allowing him to rent a room, but they had rules. And one of those rules was about to be challenged. He didn't see any way around it—not at ten o'clock at night.

Thanking the kind owners of the Model A, Clyde and Pauline made their way to the house. Normally Clyde would have let himself in, but not that night. With Pauline trembling beside him, he knocked on the door and waited.

"Why, Clyde—" Ella stopped midsentence as she opened the door and took in the sight before her.

"Ella," Clyde said soberly, "I'd like to introduce my wife."

A shocked silence followed for just a moment, and then Ella's arms opened wide as she enfolded them both in her warm and loving embrace.

"Congratulations! Come in! John, Clyde has brought home a bride! Get out some cider. This calls for a celebration!"

Later, with only congratulations and not a whisper about the "house rules," John kept Clyde occupied while Ella welcomed an emotionally drained Pauline upstairs. Kindly showing her where she could bathe and prepare herself for her husband, Ella put clean sheets on Clyde's bed so that it would be fresh for the night.

Clyde and Pauline had very little with which to begin married life, and her family didn't give them any wedding gifts, but there *was* a surprise party in their honor later that week— a wonderful wedding shower with practical gifts to help get them started. It was attended by people they didn't even know. They were all relatives of John and Ella.

• • •

Over sixty years have passed since God reached down and changed the lives of two young people named Clyde and Pauline Afman with a love that would last for generations. In those early days he blessed them by providing housing, transportation, household goods, and congratulations when they felt that no one else on earth cared about their happiness. The rift with Mama's family healed years ago, but I wish that my grandfather could have lived to see my parents go into full-time ministry. As their adult daughter, I can see that some of their choices and timing were impulsive and at times awkward; although, while growing up, I thought their story was wildly romantic! Still, God chose to protect and provide for them. I'm especially grateful that God touched their lives with the friendship of John and Ella, who planted seeds that grew into the gift of kindhearted hospitality that my parents have exhibited throughout their entire lives.

I was a stranger and you invited me in.

—MATT. 25:35B NIV

> A well-developed sense of humor is the pole that adds
> balance to your steps as you walk the tightrope of life.[1]
> —WILLIAM WARD

CHAPTER 3

The Missing Coat

BY CAROL KENT

As one of six preacher's kids, I knew how to live on a tight budget. Our family was particularly good at recycling clothing and discovering great finds at Goodwill, garage sales, and resale shops. We appreciated hand-me-downs, and all five of the girls in our family learned how to stitch up a hem and how to use a belt to make an oversized dress fit a different body type than the one for which it was designed. We had fun using a bit of trim or new buttons to give face-lifts to formerly dowdy outfits.

The most fun was when an older sister passed on a dated item of clothing—it was inevitably transformed into an outfit so unique and trendy the original owner wished she hadn't let go of it. For us it was great sport and we never realized we were poor, because we had plenty to eat, a roof over our heads, laughter, joy, and a strong spiritual foundation.

It never occurred to me until I was a married woman how much my mother sacrificed for her children. While Mama scrimped on the grocery budget so all of us could have an occasional new item of clothing, she never used those funds on anything for herself. Our needs always came before hers.

One day a woman in our small town realized that Mama needed a winter coat. She invited our mother to her home, telling her she had a special gift for her. The surprise was a coat that had belonged to the woman's mother, who had passed away fifteen years earlier. She opened a closet and removed her mother's coat, holding it to her chest as she reminisced about fond memories. The woman spoke slowly and deliberately. "I just couldn't bring myself to part with it before, but I know *you* will appreciate it. It's just like new. Mother only wore it a few times."

At first glance the coat looked promising, but when Mama tried it on, there were challenges. After spending a decade and a half in a closet, the lining, which at one time was blue, now sported purple streaks. The coat was tight across her chest, and the sleeves were much too short. The woman who cherished the coat of her elderly mother was thrilled to pass the treasured item on to our mama. Telling Mama how lovely the coat looked on her, the woman said, "I'm so pleased you will be wearing it."

Later we learned that Mama believed if she rejected the coat, it would somehow devalue the kindness and generosity with which it had been given. The memories connected to the coat made its value great to the giver. Mama thanked the woman and took the coat home.

Our mother tried to hide her feelings, but I could tell she never felt comfortable in the ill-fitting coat. Still, she wore it all winter. She had long ago learned not to complain about things she didn't like and couldn't change. I later learned the only person she ever confided in about the coat was her close friend Karen.

Another year passed, and the trees turned into their glorious fall colors. The weather was chilly, but Mama preferred a sweater to the coat. However, when the snow fell and the temperatures dipped to freezing, Mama *had* to wear a coat. She went to the closet, but that coat was nowhere to be found. Mama went through every closet in the house hunting for the coat and finally thought she must have left it on a rack in the church lobby . . . but it wasn't there either! She told Karen about the missing coat, and her friend said, "Don't worry about it, Pauline! I'm going to take you shopping for a new coat. You need one that fits you properly."

That year Mama's friend purchased a brand-new, beautiful winter coat for her. It was exactly what she needed, and it was a gift so lovely our mama never would have purchased it for herself. Mama never talked about the missing coat, but I knew she was relieved not to have to wear it anymore. And since she had worn the ill-fitting coat for an entire season, the person who provided the gift never mentioned it again.

Several years passed and our family was getting ready to move because Dad was becoming the pastor of a church in another city. As the date for our departure got closer, Karen and another friend, Janet, took Mama out for a good-bye dinner at her favorite restaurant. After the meal was served, Karen looked up with a twinkle in her eye. "Pauline, you have been a special friend to us. We want you to have this gift to remind you of how much we love you."

The gift was wrapped in a *huge* box, and Mama couldn't imagine what was inside. She opened the card and had tears in her eyes as she read the meaningful sentiments from Karen and Janet. Thanking her friends for their thoughtfulness, she carefully unwrapped the package and then folded the exquisite paper to use on a future gift. Suddenly catching a glimpse of what was inside, she *screamed*! Patrons in the restaurant were looking at her from all directions, but Mama was oblivious to the scene she was creating. Inside the box was the same coat with the purple-streaked lining that had completely disappeared several years earlier!

By this time, Karen was howling with laughter and began her hilarious confession. "I took it," she said, "knowing I planned to purchase a new one for you—but I had a problem. I couldn't figure out what to do with it. It seemed inappropriate to throw it in the garbage, so I just hung on to it." The three friends laughed until they cried.

Later, as they left the restaurant, it was mother's turn to talk. "Karen, I refuse to take that coat home with me. You will have to dispose of it yourself!" Amid additional chuckles, Karen once again took the coat home.

• • •

The time for our move to another city arrived, and we said our lingering good-byes. I knew Mama missed her friends. A few weeks later she was going through the mail and pulled out a letter from Karen. As she opened the card, a crisp five-dollar bill fell out of the envelope. Karen's note was short: "Pauline, this belongs to you. Someone recently bought *your* coat at my garage sale!"

As Mama shared this story with the family over dinner that night, she was still laughing out loud. She had been blessed twice—first with the generosity of a friend who saw her need for a coat that fit and second with the spontaneous humor that erupts out of shared experiences with a bosom buddy.

A cheerful heart is good medicine . . .

—PROVERBS 17:22 NIV

Soul meets soul on lovers' lips.[1]
—PERCY BYSSHE SHELLEY

CHAPTER 4

A Love Story

BY JENNIE AFMAN DIMKOFF

It had been my constant prayer and the longing of my heart from the time I was fifteen years old: Dear Heavenly Father, please bring me a man who will be the spiritual leader in our relationship. Please help me to recognize him and not settle for less.

I started dating early, and by my last year in high school, I knew that Mr. Right had not shown up. Although I had only dated good Christian guys, I seemed to have missed those who fell into that "spiritual leader" category. Then, unexpectedly, a letter arrived from an old friend, suggesting that we should go out.

• • •

A senior at the University of Michigan, Graydon was someone I had always been gut-level honest with. He had been my agnostic friend who hadn't believed in God, and he had loved to argue and debate with me, a minister's daughter, about religion and the *existence* of God. Although he had made fun of me for my faith, our sincere friendship had continued. Often discouraged, I had prayed for him every night for over three years until he *finally* gave his life to Jesus Christ. Since that truly amazing answer to prayer, I had found great joy in watching him grow spiritually, and the change in his life had been a tremendous boost to my own faith.

We lived over two hours apart so I hadn't been able to rejoice with him in person, but the letters we exchanged had a new, spiritual dimension that was precious to me. In one letter he had surprised me with a suggestion:

Jennie, I know you faithfully prayed for me each night. Now, it is my privilege to pray for you too. I have this idea. Why don't we pray "together" every night at eleven o'clock?

And so, across the miles, two friends had paused each night to bring one another before the Lord in prayer, each knowing that the other was praying at the very same time. However, no matter how dear our friendship was, our relationship from the very beginning had always been platonic, fun, and *comfortable*—until now.

His last letter had changed everything.

Normally, a newsy, fun, sometimes introspective letter would arrive, but the summer following his spiritual conversion, Graydon left for ROTC training camp. It was the Vietnam War era, and obviously the training had him thinking about all sorts of serious matters. To my surprise, a manila envelope arrived from the young soldier with a long letter enclosed. The contents shocked me. In essence it said,

Dear Jennie,

I am almost twenty-three years old, and I am ready to meet the girl of my dreams. For some reason, I keep thinking that she might be you. I feel awkward even making this suggestion. I've known you for years and have never even held your hand! I have had second thoughts about sending this letter, because I don't want to jeopardize the special friendship we enjoy, in case we explore this possibility and

*things don't work out. For that reason, I am leaving the ball
in your court . . . and will await your reply.*

I didn't write back for weeks. I simply did not know what to
say. Then, while doing the supper dishes one evening with my
sister, I asked out loud, "Why is it that I can talk to God about
my feelings for Graydon, but I can't seem to express them to
him?"

It was like a lightbulb turned on. Racing to my bedroom, I
pulled out a sheet of stationery and started to write.

Dear Heavenly Father,
    *I am in such turmoil. You know that I love Graydon.
But, it certainly isn't the kind of love that leads people to
marry each other. It's a love that simply grew from praying
for him night after night, and it has brought me such joy
to watch You speak to his stubborn heart and work an
amazing miracle there.*
    *I've had such a hard time responding to his letter that
I've finally decided to just talk to You about it and ask that
You communicate my feelings to him as You see fit.*

Sealing the letter, I addressed it to Graydon. The very day
he received it, he phoned, asking if he could come and see me
the first weekend his military training was completed.

• • •

During the big date I felt uncomfortable, and I was not at all
sure what to do about it. Who would have dreamed that I
would feel nervous dating one of my best friends? This was
the same guy I had known since I was in the eighth grade—
the funny, outgoing buddy I had faithfully corresponded with
after he'd left for college. I could say absolutely anything to

him in those letters. I had even asked him for dating advice!

So, there I was—sitting on the couch with my fun-loving childhood friend and feeling so awkward I could die.

"Jennie?" Graydon had turned and was looking at me intently. "Do you realize that since I've become a Christian, we've prayed together night after night from a distance, but we have never had the opportunity to actually pray *together*? Could we do that right now?"

For a moment, I felt dumbstruck. Of all the *mature* Christian guys I had dated, not one had ever suggested that we pray together on a date, and here was this new believer suggesting just that. I nodded, and Graydon surprised me further by slipping to his knees beside my parents' well-worn couch. I knelt beside him, and then, for the first time in our very long acquaintance, he reached out with a tender smile to hold my hand, bowed his head, and prayed. *Dear Lord, thank you for loving us so much. The truth is Jennie and I are feeling pretty awkward right now. You know how special our friendship is, and we don't want to jeopardize that. So, we'd like to give this relationship to you. If you just want us to be friends, then please make this the best friendship the world has ever known. If you'd like it to be more than that, well, you go right ahead and make it more.*

When Graydon finished his simple prayer, I knew it was my turn, but I could not say a word. From the moment he started praying, tears of joy had been running down my face. When no sound was forthcoming from me, Graydon opened his eyes, turned, cupped my face, and gently rubbed his thumbs over my wet cheeks. Then, while still on our knees, he pulled me into his arms and kissed me like there was no tomorrow. It was a joyful kiss. A kiss full of wonder, recognition, and promise.

Later, in contemplating why I had cried, I realized that those tears were a response from deep inside as I recognized my soul mate for the very first time. God had blessed us tenderly and joyfully. He had answered my prayer.

This is my prayer: that your love will flourish and that you will not only love much but well. Learn to love appropriately. You need to use your head and test your feelings so that your love is sincere and intelligent, not sentimental gush. Live a lover's life, circumspect and exemplary, a life Jesus will be proud of.

—PHILIPPIANS 1:9–10 MSG

Compassion brings us to a stop, and for
a moment we rise above ourselves.[1]
—MASON COOLEY

CHAPTER 5

An Unexpected Discovery in Manhattan

BY CAROL KENT

It was August of 1997, and Wendy Harrison was taking a vacation from her job as a hairdresser in Lakeland, Florida. With great expectations she boarded the plane for her first trip to New York City. She was looking forward to experiencing the sights and sounds of the Big Apple. Two and a half hours later the plane landed at LaGuardia Airport. She retrieved her luggage, headed outside, and hailed a cab. Approaching the city, she saw stately skyscrapers outlining the horizon. Gigantic billboards with neon lights beckoned her to take in Broadway productions. Wendy was mesmerized by the electricity and excitement of this bustling metropolis.

The taxi came to a halt in Times Square, near where her friend Matt had an apartment. He had moved to the big city to work as a banker and told her earlier, "This apartment is in Hell's Kitchen, so my rent is cheaper than it would be in another area." Wendy later learned this area had figured prominently in the New York City underworld three decades earlier, when it was known for being the center of organized crime. Formerly a bastion of poor working-class Irish-Americans, Hell's Kitchen had undergone a tremendous socioeconomic shift in recent days. As wealthier people bought the properties, the face of the entire area was slowly changing.

It took less than a day for Wendy to become conscious of an ever-present sound. There was a low-level hum in this multiethnic urban center that was as alive by night as it was by day. But she quickly made a more startling discovery. In stark contrast to the glitz and glamour of the city, there were less appealing sights and sounds.

One afternoon a woman wearing a Hefty bag as a dress caught her attention and yelled, "Hey, you!" Wendy gulped. She had never been exposed to this level of poverty before and realized it was easier to look away than to deal with the uncomfortable feeling of seeing so many needy people and not knowing which ones to help. Walking down the street, she peered into alleys where drug dealers were openly selling crack and cocaine. This was not the image of New York City Wendy had expected to see.

A few days later she was heading back to the apartment after a day of shopping. Looking up from an armload of packages, her eyes fell on a trendy-looking, well-dressed man in front of Times Square Church—the same church she had visited on the previous Sunday. He was cutting the hair of homeless people, and there was a long line of men waiting for their turn. The attractive man seemed out of place with this clientele. As Wendy got closer, she recognized the hairdresser as a well-known name in her industry—a star among salon owners and stylists. *What could he possibly be doing here?* she wondered.

Moved by an unseen power, Wendy put down her packages and spoke up: "Do you have an extra pair of scissors? I'm on vacation and I'm a hairdresser. It looks like you could use some help. You have people waiting, and I'd like to assist you." Following quick introductions Wendy's offer was immediately accepted and she began cutting the hair of people she never would have met under normal circumstances. As each haircut was completed, she heard a variety of comments from the unlikely recipients of an unexpected kindness:

> *"Thank you, ma'am."*
> *"I'm sorry I'm dirty."*
> *"I hope I don't smell too bad."*
> *"No one will hire me looking this way, and I couldn't afford a haircut. Thank you."*

As they finished cutting the hair of their final client of the day, Wendy asked the well-known salon owner how often he was involved in this type of service. He said, "I do this once a month. It helps homeless people to get employment, and it's my way of giving back." Shaking her hand, the gentleman handed Wendy his card as he said, "If you would ever like to have a job in my salon, I'd be honored to hire you."

Wendy thanked him, realizing she had just experienced something extraordinary—the unexpected joy that comes when you sense God's smile on your life and an approving nod from a gifted professional. There in the middle of Times Square she understood the power of compassion. It is a gift that blesses both the receiver and the giver.

You're blessed when you care. At the moment of being "care-full," you find yourselves cared for.

—MATTHEW 5:7 MSG

> The most profane word we use is "hopeless."
> When you say a person or a situation is hopeless,
> you are slamming the door in the face of God.[1]
> —KATHY TROCCOLI

CHAPTER 6

The Gift of Rosa

BY JENNIE AFMAN DIMKOFF

Chaplain Daniel had served as a hospital chaplain for about two years when he met Rosa in the ICU where he worked in Southern California. He had served as a chaplain long enough to see the myriad of tubes emanating from the hospital beds in the ICU as one of two things: a healing cocoon for some or a step toward death for others. However, when he entered the critical care unit that particular day, he had no idea the blessing he was about to receive by getting to know Rosa personally.

Rosa was a thirty-seven-year-old patient who had been born with severe birth defects that had left her with extremely limited motor skills. When she was a baby, her mother had been both neglectful and abusive, and Rosa had eventually been removed from her mother's custody. For the next seventeen years she had bounced miserably from foster home to foster home in the Chicago area.

Shortly after Rosa's seventeenth birthday, a man named Fernando Martinez died of a heart attack in San Diego, California. When his locker at the factory where he worked was cleaned out, the contents were given to his family, and among his oil-stained work effects, there was a beautiful, pristine letter from a young girl named Rosa Martinez from Chicago, who had been trying to locate her father. According to the date on the letter, Rosa's father had received the letter months before, had kept it close, but had never responded to her.

"Fernando had a daughter none of us knew about!" said his sister Maria, sharing the news with her mother and other siblings. "And the child has many special needs from the sound of this letter."

"If she is in the foster care system and she's our flesh and blood, then I think we'd better bring her home," Esmeralda, the matriarch of the family, announced.

True to their word, within just two weeks, two aunts flew to Chicago to meet Rosa and very quickly offered to bring her to live with her long-lost family in San Diego. Instead of getting a father, she got an entire family—with dozens of family members!

It turned out that Rosa was indeed a total-care person. She was bright, intelligent, and articulate, but she needed help with dressing, feeding, and bathing. She ended up living with her aunt Maria, and she had a motorized wheelchair that she skillfully operated by moving her mouth.

Despite her limitations, Rosa's spirit of adventure and desire for independence took her farther than might be expected, and Tía Maria played a helping hand. One day, Maria took Rosa to the trolley system and instructed her to get on, telling her that all she had to do was get off at the next stop. Maria promised that she would be there waiting for her. Rosa was *terrified*. She had been abused and abandoned so many times before and feared being abandoned again. But Rosa chose to trust her aunt and dared to get on that trolley.

"Oh, please be there, please be there, *please* be there!" She whispered the words over and over as the trolley approached the next stop. Her heart was thundering!

Sure enough, Tía Maria was waiting for her at the next stop.

"I did it! I did it all by myself!" Rosa yelled joyfully.

"I knew you could do it, Rosa! I knew you could! Want to do it again? Then we'll celebrate with ice cream!"

Eventually Rosa became so independent that she would run errands and do her own grocery shopping. She even had a boyfriend and, although physically unable, longed to have a family of her own.

It wasn't just her tenacious strength and vitality that so inspired her new family, though. It was also her heart. Due to her severe disability, Rosa wrote notes with a pencil in her mouth—painstakingly composing loving birthday and thank-you notes to her family and friends. For twenty years, her grateful, warm, and loving spirit became the linchpin that drew her extended family together and created a deeper family unit than they had ever been before. Thinking they were giving her the gift of a family, they had been given the gift of Rosa.

Physically fragile, Rosa had periodic health crises, and when she was thirty-seven years old, she was rushed to the intensive care unit for the last time. It was there that Chaplain Daniel had the opportunity to meet Rosa and her large family and to hear the remarkable story of her life and the impact she had made on them all.

Although a victim of abuse and neglect as a child, Rosa died an emotionally healed human being—and she died having been a healing force in a broken family, with twelve of those family members by her side when she passed away. While Rosa may not have been able to bear her own children in her lifetime, in her death she was able to give life to two other people by choosing to be an organ donor. In a way, she had her babies! While her family grieved, the gift of life that she gave to others made her death much easier for them to accept. She was God's gift not only to the Martinez family, but to two other families as well.

I quit focusing on the handicap and began appreciating the gift. It was a case of Christ's strength moving in on my weakness. Now I take limitations in stride, and with good cheer, these limitations that cut me down to size—abuse, accidents, opposition, bad breaks—I just let Christ take over! And so the weaker I get, the stronger I become.

—2 CORINTHIANS 12:9–10 MSG

God *does* care. God *does* know what He is doing. He asks us to trust Him. He asks us to remember who we are trying to understand— even when it doesn't make sense at all.[1]

—DEE BRESTIN

CHAPTER 7

Gone Too Soon

BY CAROL KENT

Our flight landed in Atlanta, and Gene and I quickly grabbed our carry-on luggage and walked off the plane. Still on the Jetway, I heard the ringtone of my cell phone, but it was buried in my purse and I needed to keep walking. Within thirty seconds Gene's phone started ringing, and I heard him say, "Hello. Who is this? I'm sorry, I can't hear you very well." Moments later, I saw Gene's ashen face. "It's your sister Paula. Tony was found dead in his apartment."

My mind swirled. *Gene must have it wrong. Our nephew is only twenty-seven years old. He can't be gone. He was getting straight A's in his university courses. He's a dynamic young man with his whole life ahead of him.* Grabbing the phone, I quickly walked through a crowd of people headed to their gates and found a slightly less congested area where I could talk to my sister. She was sobbing, and her words poured out in a cascade of emotion and incredulity.

For the past year and a half Tony had suffered from a seizure disorder and he had been in and out of the hospital. His health crisis had been compounded in recent months by a biking accident in which he broke some ribs and injured his lungs, causing a buildup of fluid that put him in the hospital again. Lately he had been much better, and we all thought he was improving. How could he be gone? But he was.

For several moments all I could do was cry with my sister.

We share a special bond—both of us are the parents of an only child. During the next few days Paula's life was filled with chaos—the police report, the autopsy, the funeral arrangements, followed by the heart-wrenching experience of sorting through her son's clothing and personal effects. I knew she was also concerned about his spiritual condition at the time of his death. She knew he had been questioning his faith. Having his life interrupted with a health crisis when he had so many hopes and dreams for the future was hard for him to accept.

A few days went by, and one evening Paula attended a celebration of her son's life in San Marcos, Texas, with the university students who knew and loved him. It was a very special time of remembering her adventurous, bright, and humorous son's life, but I also knew it was a hard night as she faced the finality of his death.

I wondered how I could best comfort my sister. My mind went back to another very difficult time in her life. Tony had been only ten years old, and Paula's marriage was ending amid a torrent of challenges. I was in western Canada for a speaking engagement when a call came from my husband: "Paula called and asked if she could fly Tony to Michigan to stay with us while she takes care of legal matters in Florida. I'm picking him up at the airport tomorrow. He'll be here when you get home."

I returned to Michigan on Sunday afternoon, just in time to attend an evening service at our church with my husband; my son, J. P.; and my nephew. I was disappointed as we entered the sanctuary, because the front of the auditorium was set up for a communion service and I didn't think Tony would understand what it meant. Once seated in the pew, I quickly got out a paper and pen for my young nephew. I was hoping he would remain distracted enough to be quiet during church. The service progressed as usual, with worship music and a sermon, followed by communion. The bread plate was passed, and I picked up a tiny, unleavened wafer and passed the plate to another parishioner seated beyond Tony and J. P.

Suddenly, Tony tugged on my arm, looked up, and said, "Oh! I know, Aunt Carol. This is the day we remember that Jesus died for us, isn't it?"

"Yes, it is, Tony. Would you like to take communion tonight?"

"Oh, yes!" he exclaimed.

The bread plate had already been passed to the next row, and all I had was a small piece of a wafer. I handed it to Tony.

Again, I felt a tug on my arm. He was holding the tiny cracker with his thumb and forefinger. "Aunt Carol," he whispered, "will you break bread with me?" That night on a church pew in Michigan, my nephew and I broke bread together and remembered that Jesus died on the cross for our sins. The grape juice was passed, and we thanked God for the gift of his son as we participated in a never-to-be-forgotten service.

I looked over at the piece of paper I had given Tony earlier. He had drawn a large cross in the center of the paper, and there were two smaller crosses on both sides. He noticed my appreciation of his artwork and spoke again. "Aunt Carol, this big cross in the middle is the one that Jesus died on. But there were bad men on the crosses on both sides of him. But one man told Jesus he was sorry for all the bad things he did and asked Jesus to forgive him. Jesus *did* forgive him and told the man he would be with him forever and ever in heaven."

After reliving the sweetness of this experience that had been tucked away in my memory for years, I called Paula and shared the story. The two of us cried together over the phone. Paula finally spoke: "You'll never know how much I needed to hear this tonight!" I knew it was a reminder of her son's early decision to invite Christ into his life, and it brought the sweet touch of comfort. We both knew Tony was finally home—out of physical pain and safely in the arms of Jesus.

All praise to God, the Father of our Lord Jesus Christ. God is our merciful Father and the source of all comfort. He comforts us in all our troubles so that we can comfort others. When they are troubled, we will be able to give them the same comfort God has given us.

—2 CORINTHIANS 1:3–4 NLT

If I cannot give my children a perfect mother,
I can at least give them more of the one they've
got . . . I will take time to listen, time to
play, time to be home when they arrive from
school; time to counsel and encourage.[1]
—RUTH BELL GRAHAM

CHAPTER 8

Miracle on Hope Hill

BY JENNIE AFMAN DIMKOFF

Life was good. Mark and Beth were young newlyweds with idyllic dreams for the future, and those dreams included having a family. Although Beth, an elementary school teacher, loved each student in her class, it wasn't long before she and Mark started trying to have a child of their own. They knew these things didn't happen overnight, but months turned into years without the longed-for, prayed-for pregnancy. Then, in the fall of 2000, Mark, a thirty-five-year-old airplane mechanic, was diagnosed with stage-three testicular cancer.

Their hopes and dreams for a child of their own were dashed, and suddenly their attention was riveted on their savior—and on survival. As friends and family prayed, Mark went through three months of rigorous chemotherapy treatments. His life was spared, but the rigors of the treatment took a severe toll on Mark's joints. By age forty, both of his hips had been replaced.

With his recovery came a new job opportunity in avionics that moved Mark and Beth closer to both of their families. They purchased their first home on Churchill Street, which was on the top of an incline, and they decided to name it Hope Hill, hoping to one day fill it with children. Investigating options for enlarging their family, they talked to several adoption agencies, only to be disappointed as they realized the cost of a traditional adoption would be prohibitive. They also looked at snowflake adoption, where they would adopt the leftover embryos of someone who had undergone in vitro fertilization and had already completed her family. Finally, they looked into foster parenting and decided to take a step of faith.

"Don't plan on adopting any of the children you foster," they were told by social services. "More than half of the time the kids go back to their own families." Mark and Beth took the required classes and became licensed, and although they realized it would be traumatic to have to give up children they became attached to, they requested placements that appeared to be long-term. They prayed over each placement the agency offered and, after being licensed for about six months, took their first one.

On January 4, 2005, Dakota, a little two-year-old boy with an unfortunate background, came into their home. With his sparkling eyes and winsome smile he captured their hearts. Beth sang him to sleep many nights those first few months, gently rubbing his back while she repeated words from an old hymn: "Take the name of Jesus with you, child of sorrow and of woe. It will joy and comfort give you, take it then where'er you go . . ."

Her voice would break as her heart was overwhelmed with thoughts of having to send this little boy away at some point in time. She thought deeply about the responsibility and privilege she and Mark had to help Dakota learn as much as possible about Jesus during the time they had with him. Beth thought about Jochebed, the mother of baby Moses in the Bible. Although Moses had been her own child, Jochebed had only a short time to teach her child all she could about God before sending him to live with unbelievers.

News came that Dakota's birth mother was pregnant again and that the baby, Dakota's half sibling, would also be placed with Mark and Beth upon birth. They took home three-day-old James from the hospital on April 1 and were informed that although Dakota was not available for adoption, it might be possible for them to adopt the newborn. The news was thrilling! This possibility brought great joy, not only to Mark and Beth, but to their extended families and to their parents, who would become grandparents to the baby. For the next two months, love and affection were poured over both Dakota and baby James.

Then came heartbreaking news. After Mark and Beth believed that the baby would be theirs, a judge decided to place him with his biological father. Devastated, they sadly prepared to give up the infant they had come to love. Their hearts were heavy, and Beth felt physically ill. So ill, in fact, that she went to the doctor. She returned home with a little pink indicator stick and shocking news that caused her heart to overflow with joy.

I'm pregnant. I'm pregnant! I am pregnant!!

What the doctors had told them was biologically impossible had happened!

The news astounded and thrilled them. In His grace, just before they had to give James up, God had blessed Mark and Beth with an unexpected, thought-to-be-impossible pregnancy. They could see God at work in their lives. That realization helped them to let go of the precious little baby they had come to love so much.

It was a roller-coaster year emotionally. As Beth's pregnancy advanced, they received news from the agency that it might be possible to adopt Dakota after all! The rights of his biological parents were being terminated, but the next weeks brought highs and lows as delays put Dakota's chance for a permanent placement on hold. Rather than dwelling on the disappointments along the way, Mark, Beth, and Dakota made wonderful memories together. A trip to the circus was great fun, but the highlight for Dakota was a rodeo with real, live cowboys! They went sledding, built snowmen, and made snow angels. Court processes continued to drag on, but in November of that year, they were finally able to officially apply for adoption.

On January 4, 2006, exactly one year to the day after Dakota came into their home, Beth gave birth to Kara, a beautiful baby girl. Two months later Dakota's adoption was finalized, and they celebrated with a party at home, which included the new grandparents and a special candle-lighting ceremony similar to the solemn but joyful promises made at a wedding. They gratefully thanked God for his double blessing.

When Dakota was five years old, he asked, "Dad, did you always wish for a son?"

"Yes, Dakota," Mark replied.

"And then God sent *me* to you," the little boy responded with obvious delight, and then added, "And you know what, Dad? I always wanted a dad just like you, and then God gave *you* to *me!*"

Our mouths were filled with laughter, our tongues with songs of joy. . . . The Lord has done great things for us, and we are filled with joy.

—PSALM 126:2–3 NIV

> Prayer lifts the heart above the battles of
> life and gives it a glimpse of God's resources
> which spell victory and hope.[1]
> —C. NEIL STRAIT

CHAPTER 9

It Happened on the Porch

BY CAROL KENT

In January of 2007, Toni's husband of twenty-eight years walked out. She found herself clinging to God like never before, aware that she was totally dependent on him to provide for her own needs, as well as those of her two children. But day after day she struggled to make ends meet.

A year and a half into the separation from her husband, she found herself in the middle of an all-day funk rehashing negative thoughts:

- *I'm overwhelmed!*
- *I'm inadequate and incapable of providing for my children.*
- *I'm taking hits from all sides—at work, at home, from the kids, and from my estranged husband.*

After spending the meager amount of money she had on a few groceries, she drove home. Suddenly and without warning, Toni began to cry—not simply dropping a few well-earned tears, but *wailing* out her grief. Her shoulders heaved uncontrollably and she could barely see the road through her torrent of grief. She felt deserted and without hope. She cried out her prayer: "God, I'm so alone. It feels like the whole world is against me. I can't function anymore. I feel like you don't care about me. I've tried hard to be a good Christian mother who cares for the needs of my children, but I'm at my wit's end. I have no one to help me. I see no way to get out from under my heavy burden, and I can't carry it anymore."

After Toni pulled up to her house, she sat in her car crying for another half hour as she continued to voice her complaints, hurts, and fears to God. Peering out the window, she looked up at a full moon. *God feels farther away from me than those stars burning in the sky millions of miles away.*

It was almost eleven PM when Toni finally pulled herself together in order to walk the few steps to her front door. While carrying a sack of groceries to her porch, Toni noticed her neighbor Maria had stopped her car right in front of Toni's house. Maria yelled out the window, "Hello!"

The friendly gesture, especially at this hour of the night, was more than a surprise. Toni hardly knew Maria. They had been neighbors for more than a decade, but they didn't really *know* each other as good friends. Toni and Maria exchanged pleasantries once in a while, but this neighbor had no idea about the difficult time Toni was currently experiencing. However, Toni *did* know that Maria was a Christian.

The streetlight by Toni's house had burned out, and it was a dark night. Toni doubted Maria would notice that she'd been crying, so she walked over to the car to return the greeting. A woman Toni had never seen before was in the passenger seat. She immediately said something in Spanish that Toni didn't understand.

Maria spoke up. "This is my sister from Costa Rica. She's a missionary to Italy and she's here visiting for a short time. She just said that God told her that you need prayer. Are you all right?"

Toni almost dropped her sack of groceries. "No, actually, Maria, I'm *not* all right."

The most sincere and kind expression came over the neighbor's face as she said, "Can we pray for you?"

Toni responded softly, "I think God sent you to do just that."

Maria parked her car and they both stepped outside. Maria told Toni to wait on the porch as she gathered the rest of the groceries from Toni's vehicle. The two women were much shorter than Toni's five-foot-eight-inch frame, and Maria's sister motioned for Toni to sit down on a porch step so they could pray over her. With kindness and compassion these two unexpected neighbors began to breathe fresh faith and renewed courage into Toni's life. Maria's sister started praying powerfully in her native Spanish while Maria translated.

Without knowing about the hopeless and discouraging day Toni had just experienced, Maria's sister placed her hands on Toni's head and said, "God says you are not alone. He is here with you." Then she placed her hands on Toni's shoulders and spoke these words: "Don't say you can't move forward. You can do *all* things through Him." Maria's sister had strong faith and spoke with a confidence in God that Toni had never before observed. This time she spoke with authority as she prayed intensely, "I bind the spirits of the enemy that are at work in this house. I pray for your children."

Her prayer was so powerful that tears welled up in Toni's eyes again. A surprising smile graced her face as she thought, *If anyone was up and about at this hour observing what just happened, it would be a neighborhood spectacle—me weeping, Maria's sister speaking loudly in a foreign language, followed by Maria's equally passionate translation.*

Finally, Maria's sister placed a hand over Toni's heart and said, "You've been bearing a large hurt for a long time, and in the name of Jesus you are released from it." Toni was startled by how much God had revealed to this stranger. Maria's sister prayed for her heavy burden to be lifted and for God's peace to fill Toni's life.

As the prayer continued, Toni stopped crying and became aware of a sweet peace invading her troubled soul. The profound weight of sadness was removed from her shoulders and she knew she could go on.

The impromptu porch prayer meeting ended, and Maria and her sister hugged Toni as they said their good-byes. As the two women got back into their car, Toni didn't fully comprehend what had just happened, but she was immediately aware of something significant. God himself had spoken clearly and personally to her through a woman she had never before met and whom she has never seen again.

As Toni entered her home, her thoughts poured out: *Everything, absolutely everything I brought before the Lord in the privacy of my car tonight was addressed through the prayer of a stranger. It was as if Maria's sister had a checklist of my concerns, and God gave them to her one by one to cross off as she prayed. I don't even know her name, but God trusted her with my need when I was desperate for help.*

Toni experienced a divine touch through the loving hands and prevailing prayer of a Spanish-speaking missionary who was listening to God's still small voice at eleven PM while she rode through her sister's neighborhood. Toni never experienced anything like this before or since. But at the time when she needed it most, God heard her desperate cry, cared about her pain, and sent a stranger to remind her of his lavish love.

For where two or three come together in my name, there am I with them.

—MATTHEW 18:20 NIV

Allow your dreams a place in your prayers and plans.[1]

—BARBARA JOHNSON

CHAPTER 10

The Bridal Gown

BY JENNIE AFMAN DIMKOFF

"Oh, Mom," I asked anxiously, "do you think it will be enough?"

"Well, it will just have to be, honey," my mother replied, "because that is *absolutely* all we can spend."

The year was 1970. I was a nineteen-year-old college student and engaged to be married. My father was the pastor of a small church and the father of six children. Finances were very tight, and I needed a bridal gown. Although he had a credit card, Dad never charged *anything* unless he knew he would be able to pay the balance in total when the bill arrived. For this very special shopping excursion, he and Mother had decided that one hundred dollars could be charged on the account, but that was absolutely the limit, and that decision had been made with great reservation.

Mother and I excitedly planned our outing, but before leaving the house she put her arms around me and prayed, asking God to bless our time together and to provide the perfect dress at just the right price.

As she finished praying, there was a knock at the door, and in walked Janet, a close friend of my mom's. She attended Mother's Bible study and went to our church. She was a lovely person, but inwardly I groaned, figuring that she would take up some of our precious shopping time with her cheerful chitchat.

After greeting her warmly, my mother explained that we were ready to go wedding dress shopping. She hoped Janet would understand that we didn't have time to visit or to have coffee that morning.

"Well, I'm glad I caught you before you left!" Janet said, smiling broadly. "I can't stay, but the Lord laid it on my heart to give you a little money toward Jennie's dress, so I'm just here to drop it off."

With that, she handed Mother a check, gave us both a quick hug, told us to have fun that day, and was on her way. Mom and I looked at each other in amazement; looked down at the check, which was written out for the amount of $25; and cheered in unison.

"Now we can spend a hundred and twenty-five dollars!"

In high spirits, we drove sixty minutes to the downtown shopping district of Port Huron, Michigan, and entered the lovely bridal salon located in Sperry's Department Store.

Our high spirits quickly dampened. Rack after rack had one thing in common. The prices were far beyond our means.

I hated to see the worry lines etched across my mother's brow, and my only real consolation was that I hadn't found a dress that had struck me as perfect. As she carefully rechecked the gowns hanging on the lone sale rack, I wandered off to look at a rack that was set off to the side. There was a gown hanging on the far end of the rack that made the breath catch in my throat. It was white satin, and it glistened with delicate seed-pearl accents. With long, tapered lace sleeves and a short, rounded train, it was exquisitely elegant.

I lifted it reverently off the end of the rack and held it against my body, just in time to see my mother coming toward me.

"Oh, Mama, *look* at this one," I whispered breathlessly. "Isn't it perfect? I just *love* it!"

In my rapture over the dress, I missed my mother's distress.

"How much is it, Jennie?" she asked cautiously, trying to keep her voice light.

"I don't know, Mom. I looked for a tag but couldn't find one."

She immediately started feeling along the neckline and sleeves for a price tag.

"There doesn't seem to be a tag on this dress." For a moment she looked at me clinging to the gown, and her voice softened. She fingered the delicate lace of one sleeve. "It really *is* a beautiful dress, honey."

She moved on to check the other dresses on the rack where I had found the gown, only to turn back in dismay.

"Jennie, these gowns must be very expensive. I can't find a price tag on *any* of them."

"Couldn't we just *ask*?" I begged, hating the despair I could see gathering in my mother's eyes.

"Ladies! May I help you?"

We turned to see the smiling department manager hurrying toward us.

"I'm sorry you had to wait! We've been so busy today!"

"Well," my mother ventured to say, gesturing toward the gown I was still clutching to my chest, "we were wondering how much *this* dress is."

"Oh, you don't want *that* dress," the clerk assured us firmly. "All the dresses on that rack have been on display in our window, and all of them need dry-cleaning." She reached out to relieve me of my treasure.

"B-but . . . but of all the dresses, this is the one that I like the very best of *all*," I responded a bit desperately. "It's just the *perfect* dress."

The woman paused and then looked from the dress to me to Mom and then back to me again.

"Why don't you go try that gown on," she said gently. "Then, if you *still* want it, and if you're willing to have the gown dry-cleaned yourself, you can have it for twenty-five dollars."

Dumbfounded, Mom and I looked at each other. Then, I whooped out a *"Yes!"* and joyfully headed for the dressing room.

Neither of us was surprised that the dress fit like it was made for me. A miracle is a miracle, after all. Not one alteration was needed. We paid for the perfect wedding gown with the $25 that God had provided that very morning, and Mother and I sang "To God Be the Glory" all the way home, recognizing that our heavenly father had indeed heard our prayer that day.

Don't worry about anything; instead, pray about everything; tell God your need and don't forget to thank him for his answers.

—PHILIPPIANS 4:6 TLB

Faith makes the uplook good, the outlook bright,
the inlook favorable, and the future glorious.[1]
—V. RAYMOND EDMAN

CHAPTER 11

A New Beginning

BY CAROL KENT

It was November of 2001. The flight from Michigan was arduous, but when we stepped off the plane on the island of Oahu, the warm tropical breezes of Hawaii quickly minimized the grueling hours of travel. The sight of tall palm trees, exotic flowers, and sugar-sand beaches immediately put us in vacation mode, and we couldn't wait to unpack and experience a swim in the Pacific Ocean, followed by local island cuisine and a romantic stroll on the beach with a view of the sunset. The best part of being on an island is that you never run out of beach. You can walk as far as your legs will take you, and there's a postcard-worthy view everywhere you look.

Gene and I arrived three days early for a women's conference at the Hawaiian Hilton Village. We were combining a brief vacation with a ministry opportunity, and we knew it would be helpful to get acclimated to the five-hour time change before the weekend event.

The conference was held on Saturday. It was a celebratory time as women gathered together from Maui, Kauai, Hawaii (the Big Island), and Oahu, and it was a special treat to meet the U.S. military wives who joined us. As delightful as the first portion of this trip had been, the best was yet to come.

A leader from one of the local island churches knew I was in town and asked if I would speak at two worship services on the following Sunday. I eagerly accepted the invitation. The casual atmosphere and the uniquely Hawaiian worship service set the tone for a glorious morning. There was a coffee break between the two services, and I noticed an attractive young woman walking in my direction. She looked professional in her crisp white blouse and navy blue skirt. It wasn't until she got closer that I noticed tears in her eyes. "Do you have a minute to talk?" she asked hesitantly.

Smiling, I reached out my hand in a warm greeting. "Yes," I said. "I'd love to talk with you." She told me her name was Stacy. The two of us filled coffee cups and found a bench in a quiet spot outside. Once we were seated, I spoke first. "Are you from this area?"

"Yes, I actually grew up on this island, and it's always comforting to come home." I noticed the tears in her eyes were now spilling down her cheeks.

"Where do you live now?" I asked.

She seemed uncomfortable with the question. "I-I'm a flight attendant for United Airlines," she stammered. "I live in Boston, and one of my regular flights was on one of the planes that crashed into the World Trade Center on September eleventh." She paused and then burst into a full-blown sob. "September eleventh was my day off work, and my friend, another flight attendant, died in my place."

For a moment I was too stunned to speak. Stacy continued. "I have been so upset that I've taken an indefinite leave from my job and come home to my native Hawaii. I'm trying to find release from my fear, and I'm trying to find God. I've never attended church regularly, but I was hoping to find answers and thought this might be a good place to start." In that moment she made direct eye contact with me and stammered, "C-can you help me?"

"Yes, Stacy, I *can* help you," I said. "What are you afraid of?"

She smiled and said, "Maybe you should ask what I'm *not* afraid of."

Over the next half hour Stacy poured out her heart. "I didn't realize how afraid I am to die until so many people lost their lives on September eleventh. Right now I'm terrorized by the thought of going back to work. I didn't know being a flight attendant could be such a dangerous job. I'm so young I thought I had a long time to get my life and faith figured out—but now I realize life is fragile and can be taken from us in a moment." Her words spilled out in a torrent of anguish.

I opened the Bible and shared with Stacy the simple truth that God loves her and sent his son, Jesus, to die on the cross for her sin and mine, and that he rose again. She listened attentively. I told her all of us need to come to a place of realizing we *need* him in our lives and we can't pick ourselves up by our own bootstraps. She said, "That's me! I am out of options for fixing my own life."

That morning as we sat on a bench with sand under our feet and ocean breezes blowing through our hair, Stacy prayed a simple prayer and invited Christ into her life. As she looked up, her face was radiant. "Thank you," she said. "I know this is a new beginning in my life, and a huge weight has been lifted off my shoulders."

It was time for the second service to begin, and my new friend hugged me before she left. That morning, Stacy experienced a divine surprise, the sweet comfort of faith, the kind of faith that dispels fear and provides the assurance of a future in heaven.

Do not be afraid, for I am with you . . .

—ISAIAH 43:5 NLT

> Dear God, it's me and it's urgent.[1]
> —MARION STROUD

CHAPTER 12

The Unexpected Angel

BY JENNIE AFMAN DIMKOFF

"Okay, girls, you had too much fun with that last discussion question. We need to move on to the next!"

Laughter erupted once again in my sister Bonnie's living room. The women at the neighborhood Bible study were bonding, and it was only the second meeting. Bonnie had invited every woman for two blocks and beyond, and she was leading the study in her home, just four doors down from my house. I had donated the books and was covering those evenings and our precious neighbors with prayer.

Bonnie went on. "The question is, do you ask God for help on a regular basis? And when was the last time you specifically saw God answer one of your prayers?"

Chris Polanski spoke up first.

Our neighbor Chris was a darling, tiny, five-foot-tall, seventy-three-year-old woman who bubbled with laughter and made everyone around her feel special. Her home was a historic, three-story, red brick Georgian colonial that was a showstopper on the Christmas home tour, and her collection of rare antiques and taste in decorating made it a treat to be invited to step inside. She and her husband, Joe, had been married for fifty years before he passed away. Joe had been sick for over ten of the last years of their marriage, and Chris had been his caregiver. It had been rough, and for the last two years of his life, he no longer recognized his children or grandchildren, which had been heartbreaking for both her and their kids.

"How do you keep on going, Chris?" I once asked her.

"I just do," she told me quite matter-of-factly. "I love my Joe, and I made a promise before God when I got married that it would be for better or for worse." Then her eyes sparkled and she laughed. "But it better not get any worse than this!"

It *had* gotten worse. However, even as neighbors, we never realized until that night in Bible study how hard Chris's situation sometimes was—and how kind and gracious God had been to her during a time of desperate need.

"I can tell you about God answering a prayer of mine," Chris announced to the group. "I'll never forget it as long as I live.

"This isn't a pretty story, but taking care of the sick sometimes isn't," she said sadly. "Late in Joe's illness he had no control over his bodily functions, and due to his large size and me being so small, it was, at times, a terrible challenge for me to change his disposable underwear. One afternoon I had him on the portable commode in the downstairs sitting room, and I unstrapped the underwear only to find a horrible mess. I needed to lift him so that I could clean him up, and I struggled and struggled but it only made matters worse! I was so tired and discouraged, and I threw back my head and silently cried, *Dear God! Please help me!*

"Just moments later, while I was still struggling to lift Joe, I heard someone open the front door and call, 'Hallooo . . . Hallooo . . . I heard your call for help. What do you need me to do?'

"I was shocked! It was a woman's voice, but no one had rung the doorbell."

Chris explained that it was the papergirl, standing just outside the door with her head peeking inside. Actually, Barb was well-known in the area as a woman who delivered papers in the neighborhood, in addition to doing odd jobs and yard work, and always had a smile on her face.

Chris went on with her story. "I went to the door and asked her what she was talking about.

"She responded, 'I was across the street delivering papers, and I heard you call out for help. So, here I am. What do you need me to do?'

"At first I was just shocked that she was there," Chris said. "She had been across the street, and I hadn't said anything *out loud* at all! Plus, the mere thought of involving anyone else in so personal a mess was mortifying," she added. "However, I was desperate for help, and Barb was right there. Without a doubt, God had sent her as an answer to my prayer, but before I invited her inside, I needed to warn her about the horrible mess, and I explained what my situation was. I told her, 'If you could just lift my husband up, I'll clean up everything below.'

"Do you know what that angel said to me that day?" Chris asked our group. "Barb said, 'No problem, Mrs. Polanski. I used to help my dad like that all the time. He was disabled before he died. And don't you worry about the smell. I can help you today.'"

Bonnie got up to get a box of tissues to pass around the room, because Chris wasn't the only one who was weeping as she finished her touchingly honest account of what had happened. Chris's story was one of the first that bonded that group of neighborhood women, reminding us all that God not only specializes in hearing the cry of our hearts and answering our prayers, but that he delights in using very special people to meet our needs right when we need it most.

Cast all your anxiety on him because he cares for you.

—I PETER 5:7 NIV

> You were planned for God's pleasure . . . You exist for
> his benefit, his glory, his purpose, and his delight.[1]
> —RICK WARREN

CHAPTER 13

Chasing an Elusive Dream

BY CAROL KENT

On the day of our son's birth I was filled with awe. This tiny, five-pound, fourteen-ounce baby was entrusted to us five years after we married. Gene and I were committed to nurturing his potential and helping him discover his calling and purpose in life.

As Jason grew, he loved everything military—GI Joe, dressing in camouflage, collecting survival gear, and building a fort in the woods behind our house. Years later he wrote:

> I wanted to be a military man for as long as I can remember. Once I visited the United States Naval Academy, I knew that becoming a midshipman in Annapolis, Maryland, would be my goal. Throughout high school I participated in all kinds of extracurricular activities, enrolled in the most difficult academic classes, earned varsity letters in sports, and strove to the best of my ability to groom myself into what I thought would be an ideal candidate for selection.

I watched as our son set his goal and began engaging in the academic work and physical exercise that would prepare him to achieve success. Pursuing this dream required that he undergo a tough screening process that demanded high achievement, community service, and athletic excellence. It culminated in interviews with congressional staffers. Jason knew the only

mechanism of entry was to first receive a nomination for can-
didacy from one of our Michigan congressmen or senators,
and he knew the field of applicants was long and deep.

He explained what happened next:

I grew a lot during the years of preparation as I challenged
myself in the classroom as never before, embraced the
risks of running for elective office, and gave it my all on
the athletic field. I also had to request recommendations
from teachers, and their letters of affirmation exceeded
my expectations. My guidance counselor said I was the
most competitive candidate he had ever recommended. I
was grateful for such encouragement and excited about
watching my dreams come true after so much hard work and
preparation.

In early December of 1992 I went out to the mailbox and
sifted through a stack of advertisements and letters. An em-
bossed envelope addressed to my son caught my attention:
HOUSE OF REPRESENTATIVES, WASHINGTON, DC. My heart skipped
a beat and I could hardly wait for him to get home from school.

When Jason tore open the envelope, he discovered a letter from Congressman David Bonior saying, "I am pleased to
inform you that I have nominated you as a candidate for the
class entering the United States Naval Academy in the summer
of 1993. The Academy will now select the appointees from
among the people I have nominated. The Academy will consider your complete record. I want to congratulate you on the
achievements which led to your nomination . . ."

A few months went by, and we heard from the families of
several other Michigan-based students who had received nomi-
nations from their elected officials. Their sons and daughters
had already been notified of appointments. As month followed

month, Jason waited—but he did not receive the hoped-for letter of acceptance.

I watched my son go through high school graduation with many honors. Relatives and friends gathered at a large open house in his honor, but I could see the sadness in his eyes. He made backup plans to go to another university, but I knew his dream of becoming a midshipman at the U.S. Naval Academy was shattered. Jason later wrote:

> We all graduated and summer began. I was left wondering why I wasn't invited to "the big dance" after God had miraculously worked out so many things in my favor in previous months. Graciously, my relatives invited me to join them for a weekend of adventure at an amusement park in a nearby state. I eagerly looked forward to the break from my preoccupation with preparation for the Academy and from second-guessing my decisions. It was good to relax and have fun with my cousins.
>
> While camping at the park, I couldn't sleep and walked along the beach in the middle of the night. I found myself opening my heart to God and talking to him about the situation. As I prayed out loud, I shared all my hopes, dreams, and frustrations regarding all of the effort put into the pursuit of my goal that now appeared more than impossible.

Jason thanked God for the many supportive people who had offered advice and tangible help. He acknowledged the privilege of receiving the initial nomination, even though it didn't land him the longed-for appointment. As he continued to pray, he said, "Lord, I accept your will for my life." Then something clicked spiritually in my son's heart like never before. He later said:

I realized that God alone knew what was best for me and that he'd obviously decided Annapolis wasn't it. God had shut the door that seemed to have opened earlier in the year. I had peace about that, and for the first time in my life I trusted God and his plan as best. As hard as it had been to accept, if his plan didn't include the navy, then so be it. I was through striving, and instead I would wait for his lead regarding what was next on my life path. I finally let go of my dream and released it to God.

Jason enjoyed a lot of relaxing laughter and fun with his cousins during the rest of the trip before returning home. But something had happened in his absence that included a surprise he wasn't expecting.

Gene and I met Jason outside as the van pulled into the driveway. A call had come from Annapolis while he was away. I had answered the phone. "Ma'am," the woman said in a matter-of-fact tone, "if your son received an appointment to the U.S. Naval Academy at this late date, would he still be interested in accepting it?" I could hardly breathe.

"Would he accept it?" I asked incredulously. "He'd be on the first plane to the East Coast! He would be *thrilled* to accept an appointment! This opportunity has been his dream for several years." Jason later marveled over what had transpired.

That weekend, when I accepted God's direction for my life, I accepted the fact that he was closing the door for me to join the navy as a midshipman in Annapolis. But God had a big surprise in store for me! The very same day I surrendered to him, the Academy came calling, asking if I was still interested in receiving an appointment.

Mom shared how they knew it was late to be asking, but they had a slot for me to fill, if I was still interested. They

told her everything would have to happen quickly with the
paperwork because plebe summer started in two weeks.
Mom asked why they were calling at such a late date. They
replied that in their office that morning they kept returning
to my file. It was as if my application jumped out at them
during their deliberations on the final appointments, so they
were making their offer now.

Two weeks later my son had a shaved head and a navy uniform, and he embarked on a whole new way of life. Jason soon discovered that the Academy is arduous and exhausting with athletics, academics, and an overall stress load so intense he contemplated quitting almost nightly during his first six months. But he had experienced God's powerful direction— and Jason knew he could make it if he continued to persevere. A few years later he wrote:

What kept me there was the path of my arrival and
acceptance. Because I knew God's hand was on it, I knew
I was where he wanted me to be, so I persevered. I saw his
purpose and mission and placement. If I'd been accepted
earlier like other midshipmen and not via such miraculous
circumstances, I would have most assuredly quit within the
first few weeks and would never have made it through the
tough days and nights.

I might have then followed a pattern of quitting
whenever anything got a little too difficult, but God knew
that and graciously nudged me to follow a different plan—
his plan, a much better plan. He orchestrated events that
allowed me to grow. I grew spiritually as I surrendered to
him at the lake; later, I grew mentally and academically as I
endured those intensely difficult four years at the USNA.

After God moved in my son's life, I watched a transformation take place. Jason puts it this way:

With God's help, I learned to thrive in the midst of the pressure of academic demands and military life, but more important, I learned to be grateful for God loving me enough to bless my life's dream with an open door.

People may make plans in their minds, but the Lord decides what they will do.

—PROVERBS 16:9 NCV

I have been driven to my knees many times by the overwhelming conviction that I had nowhere else to go. My own wisdom, and that of all about me, seemed insufficient for the day.[1]

—ABRAHAM LINCOLN

CHAPTER 14

Emergency Radio Broadcast

BY JENNIE AFMAN DIMKOFF

"Maxine?" Rizz's voice over the phone line sounded desperate. "Have you heard anything from your sister? Do you have any news about our son, Joe, and his family?"

"We've had no news at all today, Rizz. I'm so sorry."

The year was 1971, and Maxine and Fred Carlson lived in Newberry, Michigan, where Fred was a pastor. E-mail had not yet been invented, and Rizz DeCook phoned often to check for any tidbit of information they might have received. Maxine's sister, Eleanor, and her husband, Jay Walsh, were serving as missionaries in the southern part of East Pakistan with Rizz's son, Dr. Joe DeCook, and his wife, Joyce.

The Walshes had arrived in 1960, pioneering the tribal ministry that, in 1964, became part of Memorial Christian Hospital at Malumghat. The DeCooks had arrived to join the hospital's medical staff in 1970. Joe's parents, both nonbelievers, found it very difficult to understand how their brilliant son could have taken their four precious grandchildren to live half a world away in that remote and primitive war-torn country.

There had been plenty of things to be concerned about regarding the safety of their families that year, and it would often be days or weeks before they would know if their loved ones were safe. This caused anguish for all of them, but especially for a mother who did not have the savior to turn to for comfort.

First, there had been a cyclone of epic proportions. Then the Pakistani general election made it clear that the people of East Pakistan wanted their independence, and in 1971, civil war had broken out. In response, troops were deployed by the government of Pakistan, who, as Jay wrote, "crisscrossed East Pakistan on a brutal killing, raping, and burning campaign. The nine months of genocide that followed left over three million Bengalis dead. That suppressive campaign became a threat to the safety of all missionaries living in the land, given their assumed loyalty to East Pakistan. On March 26, 1971, Bengali leaders declared that as of that date, Bangladesh was a sovereign and independent nation. This only further inflamed the Pakistani troops."[2] Jay later wrote that it seemed as if all hell had broken loose.

By this time, thirty-one missionaries, including the Walshes and the DeCooks, lived and worked at the Memorial Christian Hospital. They were well aware that if Pakistani troops marched their way, they would be in extreme danger.

In preparing for that worst possible scenario, the missionaries had organized an evacuation committee, which identified three possible routes for escape. Each would be extremely dangerous, and the missionaries agreed that they would not evacuate unless the Lord gave them a specific sign to do so.

• • •

On April 20, 1971, Rizz DeCook went to the Carlsons' home in Newberry, Michigan, to see if they had heard anything about the missionaries. Tension had mounted as the families had heard of the violence and bloodshed that was taking place in East Pakistan.

"I'm so sorry, Rizz. We haven't received any new information in days. There's been no mail and nothing over the short-wave radio from the Voice of America." Maxine reached out to her friend, wishing she could comfort her more. "We simply *must* trust God to take care of them."

Rizz left in a state of high anxiety.

Sighing heavily, Maxine closed the door and started praying as she turned back to her ironing. She was deeply burdened for her friend, and she begged God to give them some word soon for this mother who didn't know his comfort. Her heart was heavy, and as she worked, she poured out her heart to her Lord.

Reaching to hang a crisply ironed shirt on the rack beside her, Maxine happened to glance at the clock and she noted the time. It was one PM.

Although they hadn't received a message on the shortwave radio in days, she decided to try again, tuning to the Voice of America just in case she could catch the signal.

Within seconds, she was shocked to hear a message: *"This is a special announcement from Washington to American citizens at Malumghat, East Pakistan. All nonessential personnel should proceed immediately via motor vehicle, using four-wheel drive, to the Burma border. The route to Chittagong is no longer available. I repeat . . ."* This meant that Pakistani troops were already moving south from Chittagong toward Malumghat!

Maxine fell to her knees, thanking the Lord, but she was afraid that she might have misunderstood. Then, as she knelt there on the floor, the message was repeated! In fact, it was repeated several times in the next few minutes. Maxine calculated that it was now just after eleven PM in East Pakistan, and it was possible that no one might be awake to hear the message!

She cried out in prayer. "Oh, God, *please* get this message to these dear ones immediately and keep them safe as they evacuate! I am half a world away and can do nothing except leave this in your hands, but I believe that you can do anything!"

Mobilized now, she called her husband at the church office to call families and supporting churches to start their prayer chains. Then she ran down the street to the home of a neighbor where she knew Rizz would be. When she told Rizz about the announcement, the women cried together. Then Rizz left to buy her own shortwave radio.

That critical message had come through as a miraculous answer to Maxine's prayer, but it was the last VOA message the Carlsons would receive on their shortwave radio for days.

• • •

It had been a long night, and after helping with an emergency surgery, Becky Davey, director of nursing at Memorial Christian Hospital in Malumghat, returned to her room in the medical compound. Normally the governmental electrical supply turned off by ten PM, but for some reason the power was still on. Although she seldom listened to the radio, she tuned in to the Voice of America as she prepared for bed. It was eleven PM on Tuesday, April 20.

Following the eleven fifteen news summary she was startled to hear, *"This is a special announcement from Washington to American citizens at Malumghat . . ."* Wasting no time, Becky rushed out to wake the others in the compound, knocking on their bedroom windows and spreading the news.

Jay Walsh, Maxine Carlson's brother-in-law, called everyone together. The group agreed that this was God's sign telling them the time had come to evacuate. Deciding to send their families ahead with the others, two senior medical staffers would stay behind to cover medical emergencies and to try to protect the Bengali staff and property.

Dr. Viggo Olsen later wrote, "The government electric supply always turned off promptly at ten PM. That night the lights stayed on until four AM, allowing the frantic families time to finish packing. At six AM on April 21, four Land Rovers with U.S. flags flying, each loaded with twenty-nine departing Americans and their luggage, headed south toward Burma."[3]

In the days that followed, God protected the missionary evacuees as well as the doctors at Malumghat in supernatural ways. While many prayed faithfully on the other side of the world for their safety, they survived terrifying experiences that would have cost them their lives if it had not been for God's miraculous protection. The missionaries were later able to return to their hospital compound, located in a new nation: Bangladesh.

• • •

God unmistakably reached down and touched Maxine Carlson in answer to her plea for a word of news to share with her friend, prompting many to immediately pray for those at the mission compound in East Pakistan. On the other side of the world, he answered those prayers. It was no accident that Becky Davey had assisted with emergency surgery that night and was up late. Nor was it a coincidence that the electricity had stayed on, that she had an unusual desire to listen to the news, or that she would hear the last Voice of America evacuation announcement made and that the missionaries evacuated safely. God's loving care and hand of protection was clearly evident on April 20, 1971, and his touch literally spanned the globe.

———————

Then they cried out to the Lord in their trouble,
and he brought them out of their distress . . . He
guided them to their desired haven.

———PSALM 107:28, 30 NIV

———————

Peace is the deliberate adjustment of
my life to the will of God.[1]
—EDWARD G. BULWER

CHAPTER 15

Escorted by Angels

BY CAROL KENT

The call was unusual. My father-in-law asked if we could come for a visit, simply saying, "I have something to tell you that I'd rather say in person. Can you make the trip to St. Helen this weekend?"

We had a busy schedule and I wasn't very excited about traveling to Northern Michigan for an unknown reason. My husband and I had been married for two years, and we were teaching school in different districts. Our short time together on weekends was precious.

Gene tossed our luggage into the trunk, and we began the three-hour drive. As we turned onto I-75, I spoke up. "I wonder what is so important that Dad felt he needed us with him in person to share the news." Then, for the first time since the call, a frightening thought entered my mind. *I wonder if Dad has been diagnosed with a serious illness. Could he be dying, and he didn't want to tell us over the phone?*

Those thoughts had obviously already hit Gene, because he simply nodded when I expressed my thoughts out loud. "I know," he muttered. "Dad is never this serious, and I don't ever recall a time when he insisted we drive so far for a last-minute family meeting."

With somber faces, we knocked on the door, and Dad and his wife, Donna, greeted us warmly. Dad certainly didn't *look* sick. In fact, he appeared to be in high spirits. His eyes twinkled as he poured lemonade and asked us to sit down in the family room. He lovingly caressed Donna's back as he asked the usual questions:

> *"How was the trip north on the freeway?"*
> *"Did you run into bad traffic?"*
> *"Are you both enjoying your teaching jobs?"*
> *"How long do you think you'll continue working as youth directors at the church?"*

We responded to each of the questions, but we sensed this meeting was arranged for a much more important reason than catching up on our day-to-day activities.

Finally, Dad spoke up. "Well, you're probably wondering why I asked you to come on such short notice. I won't keep you in suspense any longer. Donna and I have just found out we are expecting a baby, and we wanted to tell you before you got the news from someone else."

My husband is usually a dynamic conversationalist, but he was suddenly speechless. Gene was twenty-four years old and he was about to get an unexpected sibling. "W-w-w-wow!" my husband blurted out. "Congratulations to both of you! This is definitely a big surprise!"

The rest of our visit was filled with the joy of anticipating a child. Neither Dad nor Donna was expecting to conceive a baby, but it happened—and they were thrilled. They were almost giddy with the delightful thought of bringing a new baby home from the hospital. It didn't take long for the entire extended family to begin anticipating the birth.

Lori came into this world on a clear, sunshiny day. From the beginning, her presence in a room always made the atmosphere brighter. I was sure I saw her smile when she was still an infant, but when you have a vivid imagination, a baby's

gas often produces a facial contortion that can easily be inter-
preted as a legitimate smile.

As Lori grew, she seemed to have trouble breathing; she
coughed a lot and had frequent lung infections. Medical tests
revealed that my young sister-in-law had an inherited disease
called cystic fibrosis. This vicious disorder affects the respira-
tory and digestive systems, along with the sebaceous glands
and the pancreas. Within a short time, the negative aspects
of the disease began to wreak havoc on Lori's tiny body. Her
lungs produced thick, sticky mucus that kept her from breathing normally and often blocked her bowel, producing great
discomfort.

Following the diagnosis, Lori began an intense regimen of
treatments. There were often debates about whether or not to
put Lori through more rigorous procedures when she was in
obvious discomfort. By the time she was eight, this lung-wasting
disease had to be treated with drugs that produced a barrel chest
and a huge belly on her tiny, thirty-two-pound body. Lori was
always a little lady, and she struggled with not feeling as pretty
as she had once been. The steroids made her face swell, and the
tips of her fingers became like large blue pads.

The disease attacked like a predator, and young Lori made
a choice. She determined not to give in to the depression and
the discouragement of a terminal illness. Her voice was chip-
per as she joked with her physicians: "You know, Doctor, I'm
going to charge *you* for this visit. If you go through with this
examination, you'll owe me fifty cents!" The doctors loved
Lori and often lingered long after the examinations were over.
Being in her presence was a gift of life, love, and peace.

When I walked into Lori's room, she would often be lying
on an elevated board in order to drain her lungs and improve
her breathing. When I tried to comfort her, I'd hear Lori's
sweet voice say, "Don't worry about it. I'll be okay." Her laugh-

ter could be heard in every corner of the house. She often joked with her siblings and joined in the fun of each moment.

During the next two years Lori's physical condition grew progressively worse. I walked in one afternoon, and my now ten-year-old sister-in-law looked up and smiled. "Hi, Carol. I'm so glad you came. I've been talking to God a lot lately, and I'll be going to see him soon."

"What makes you think *that?*" I asked, with fresh tears trickling down my cheeks.

"I just know," she said with a smile. "It's almost time, and it's okay."

That day God touched us both with peace that can only be explained supernaturally. There was an angelic glow around this precious child. Her facial expression exuded the quiet confidence that God was in control of her destiny and that even if her life was short, it had been a great ride. I felt comforted and calm as her peaceful spirit impacted my own response to her condition.

Lori was with her parents a few days later when God called her home. A smile outlined her lips as she took her last breath. Lori's arms were raised upward. Dad said, "It was as if angels had come to carry her safely into the arms of Jesus."

I am leaving you with a gift—peace of mind and heart. And the peace I give is a gift the world cannot give. So don't be troubled or afraid.

—JOHN 14:27 NLT

I could go through this day oblivious to the miracles all around me or I could tune in and "enjoy."[1]

—GLORIA GAITHER

CHAPTER 16

The Convention Catalog

BY JENNIE AFMAN DIMKOFF

I was a minnow in an ocean.

My heart pounded wildly as I walked across the vast convention floor searching through the maze of kiosks and publishers' booths for a company called Spring Arbor. It was my very first book signing, and I didn't want to be late. I was new to the book industry, and my knowledge of publishers and distributors was sorely limited. I assumed this Spring Arbor company was associated with Spring Arbor University, a small Christian school in Michigan. Since I was from Michigan myself and had recently taken a class offered by that particular university, I assumed they had kindly invited a recent, fifty-year-old student to sign books at their booth.

Seeing the banner just ahead, I breathed a sigh of relief and reached out a hand to greet the woman who was approaching me with a broad smile on her face.

"Hello, Jennie! We're all set for you."

The woman indicated that I should sit on a stool, handed me a pen, and explained that she would hand me books one at a time as I signed them for people who were lined up waiting for their copy.

Thirty minutes later, I signed the last book and surrendered the stool to another author who was waiting in the wings. I turned to my hostess to thank her for her assistance.

"Jennie, would you like one of our catalogs?" she asked.

I nodded politely and reached for the proffered Christian Book Association convention issue of *The Christian Advance,* only to be startled to see *my* book, *Night Whispers,* featured all by itself in living color on the front cover of the publication.

"That's my book," I blurted in surprise.

"I know." The woman nodded with a smile. "We picked it for the front of this issue. It's featured on the inside as well. Congratulations!"

"Wow," I responded, and then asked a little sheepishly, "Could I have an extra copy for my mom?"

She smiled and graciously handed me two.

Later, I was dumbfounded to learn that Spring Arbor Distributors had absolutely no affiliation with the Michigan university, that it was one of the largest Christian book distributors in the world, and that my publisher had no prior knowledge of the placement of my book in the distributor's catalog. Furthermore, I was humbled beyond all measure when I realized the long-awaited *The Message* Bible was advertised on page two of the catalog, and Oliver North's latest novel was featured on the back cover!

Impossible. How had my lowly book ended up on the cover of such an influential publication? Bottom line, it should *not* have happened. Absolutely nothing I could have done, orchestrated, arranged, or manipulated through my own lowly contacts could have resulted in that magazine cover.

Pure and simple, God had reached down and blessed me.

As I marveled over this phenomenon I was reminded of an e-mail that had arrived the day before I left for the convention. It was from my friend Patsy Clairmont, a well-known author and speaker on the Women of Faith tour whom I had known since I first started speaking. She knew better than I did how exciting it would be to have my first book released at the convention and to be a featured speaker at a promotional event put on by my publisher. Every word of her e-mail was meaningful to me. She wrote:

> *Dear Jennie,*
>
> *I will pray for your "coming out" at CBA. What fun! Enjoy the experience—God has long been at work preparing you—all you have to do is lean forward and pour out his living word. . . . You are a refreshing gift to the body. I hope your time there will be full of sweet surprises. I'm in your corner cheering!*
>
>

Love,

Patsy
>

I recalled with wonder what had happened as I reread her e-mail. Sweet surprises, indeed! I had experienced unearned, unmerited favor from God.

Sometimes I get so caught up with the busyness or tenseness of my circumstances that I forget that life is full of God moments and unexpected blessings. There have been several times in my past when those blessings have shocked and surprised me. Other times those blessings came as direct answers to specific prayers. I am trying to learn to savor those moments, to revisit the memories, and most important, to remember to say thank you to the one who loves me most.

May the Lord continually bless you with heaven's blessing as well as with human joys.

—PSALM 128:5 TLB

We can't remake our pasts. But with God we can
handle the past . . . No matter what has happened
in our backgrounds, with God there is grace, peace,
and hope if we'll run to Him and bring every past
disappointment captive to faith in His Word.[1]

—KAY ARTHUR

CHAPTER 17

A Different Kind of
Fairy Tale

BY CAROL KENT

It was Missy's daughter's fifteenth birthday. Suddenly, she blurted out, "Mom, I don't want Dad around. I want him out of the house when my friends come for my party!"

Missy's husband, a pastor for over twenty years, had recently confessed his marital unfaithfulness to his wife, and he had been asked to leave his ministry. Their family was in chaos, trying to make sense out of the unfathomable—a good husband and father who had been a committed Christian, swept into a vortex of lies and deceit.

She and her husband had experienced great joy, along with difficult struggles, during their ministry. Now trials and frustration were piled upon disappointment and mistrust until both of them were drowning in a sea of hurt, confusion, and unspeakable personal and public humiliation for themselves and their children.

When Missy's husband first confessed his adultery to her, it was so far removed from the person she believed him to be that she thought he was joking. As the shock of his words and the penetrating reality of what he had done finally made their way to her consciousness, she ran and hid in a closet. During her growing-up years, the confines of a closet had been her refuge as a child living in a volatile home situation. But she was no longer a child, and God had brought her far enough along the road to inner healing that she didn't stay in that closet very long. However, she quickly left the house in a panic and raced to the home of friends for comfort and advice.

Missy felt like she was living in a nightmare. When she finally calmed down enough to return home, her husband was waiting for her in their bedroom. As Missy entered the room, she ranted, "You have destroyed our lives! You've taken away our livelihood! My whole world is in shambles because of your selfish choices! You have lied to me, made a fool of me, and betrayed me!"

After the abuse she had experienced as a child, this new pain ran too deep for words. Knowing she had every right to throw him out of the house, walk away, and never forgive him, she yelled, "Get out! Get out of this bedroom! Get out of this house! Get out of my life!"

The world as Missy knew it crashed down around her. Later, she explained, "My trust was shattered; my children were in turmoil; my marriage was crushed. The devastation was beyond anything I could ever imagine. All I had believed in, all we as a family stood for, and all we had sacrificed felt like a sham."

But in the billowing cloud of carnage and rubble and the disintegration of all she had thought to be true, one thing had not been crushed. Her heart was firmly planted in God's word. That year Missy had specifically been praying two verses. One was from Philippians 3:10: "I want to know Christ—yes, to know the power of his resurrection and participation in his sufferings, becoming like him in his death."[2] The other verse she had been focusing on was from 1 Peter: "He did not retaliate when he was insulted, nor threaten revenge when he suffered. He left his case in the hands of God, who always judges fairly."[3]

When she paused long enough to listen, she heard God's quiet voice say, "My child, if you walk away now, it will be all over. It will be too late for me to show you what I can do with your life and marriage if you yield it to me."

Her husband was gathering his things as he prepared to leave. With a clear knowledge of the long journey that lay ahead of them if they were going to move in the direction of reconciliation and forgiveness, she found unexpected words coming out of her mouth: "Stop! Don't go."

• • •

Being honest with their children about what had happened was difficult, but it was essential if they were ever going to move past this deep betrayal and begin the long road to healing. Their sons were eighteen and seventeen, and their daughter was just turning fifteen years old. Missy wondered if anger would tempt them to rebel against their father and turn their backs on God. They had been taught biblical principles throughout their growing-up years, but now, in the face of their father's huge failure, how would they respond?

Missy's husband committed himself to the process of restoration and accountability. Missy, still feeling the pangs of betrayal, committed herself to "the one who judges righteously." It was difficult. Progress was not instant. The children watched their dad and mom walk a difficult path toward healing. Their oldest son said, "Dad, if your repentance is real, it will last. But if you are trying to change on your own, it won't work." Over time, the children watched, waited, and made their own steps toward forgiveness.

Missy's thoughts were jumbled. She later said, "I remember thinking that life, as we knew it, was over. We had lost much— so many dreams would be unfulfilled. What would our future look like? Could we remain together as a family?" The children struggled, and sometimes Missy thought things wouldn't work out, but they persevered.

She was right about one thing—their old life *was* over. But as time passed, Missy was surprised to find new life on the other side of a broken relationship. As a couple, their relationships with God, each other, and their children deepened as they experienced emotional and spiritual healing.

Missy discovered something significant. Not only were they experiencing personal wholeness and restoration, they were enveloped in an unexpected burst of joy for all God had done for them as a family. Through Missy's journey of healing from childhood abuse and brokenness, God had prepared her to be a vessel of forgiveness for her husband. Each difficult step in the process, each issue of pride and sin that was laid before God, and every obedient move forward brought new life to their marriage and to their family.

• • •

Seven years later, Missy was living in the middle of a dream she once thought would be impossible. It was her daughter's wedding day. Missy explained what took place: "My precious little girl, now grown, was the princess in the fairy tale—a beautiful bride arriving in a white horse-drawn carriage on the arm of her father. She once again looked up at her daddy with love, admiration, and trust."

After they walked together down the aisle, Missy's husband handed his daughter to her groom and then turned around to perform the marriage ceremony. Tears of gratitude filled the eyes of the entire wedding party—including Missy's sons and their wives, along with family members and friends who had walked with them through a difficult time. That day everyone celebrated God's touch of reconciliation and the joy that comes when we walk in his ways.

———————————

Restore to me the joy of Your salvation,
And uphold me by Your generous spirit.

—PSALM 51:12 NKJV

———————————

> **Waste not, want not.**
> —AUTHOR UNKNOWN

CHAPTER 18

Grandma No No

BY JENNIE AFMAN DIMKOFF

I had a mean grandmother. Most of my friends have wonderful grandmother stories, but not me. Grandma Gertrude was my adversary. I dreaded when she came to visit. Whenever she came, the Afman children were tidied up and lined up to kiss her cheek and "welcome" her to our home. My dutiful peck was scrubbed off my lips with the back of my hand the moment her back was turned.

She was a small, wiry woman who leaned forward and strutted purposefully when she walked. She always wore a dark dress, and her ankles were thrust into matronly tie-up, black shoes. When I was little, I thought her calves resembled small turkey drumsticks.

Grandma Gertrude didn't believe in spoiling her grandchildren by giving treats, giving Christmas gifts, or remembering birthdays. What she did insist on was that we eat our vegetables, and Grandma Gertrude was partial to canned peas. I can remember those days like yesterday.

The spoon loomed closer. At eye level now, it swam before my eyes. My stomach roiled as the smell of canned peas overwhelmed me. Bile rose in the back of my throat. Just as the grip of steely fingers fastened themselves around my chin . . .

. . . I woke with a start! Relief flooded over me. It had been a dream. As I lay back and drew a tremulous breath, the reality of what had prompted the nightmare came to me. She was coming today. Grandma Gertrude was coming for a whole week—and she always brought canned peas.

"Jennie Beth, wake up, honey! You'll be late for the bus. You have to eat your breakfast and get into your Halloween costume. You don't want to miss your party!" Mother's voice was too cheerful after a night filled with pea-green dreams, but I groggily dragged myself downstairs and eventually got caught up in the excitement of the day. Mother brushed my long hair and fitted a wide white band with a hand-stitched red cross over my head. She had made my costume herself just the day before, and I loved it.

"You are going to be the prettiest eight-year-old nurse in the whole world," Mother assured me with a kiss. Her huge stomach bulged between us, and I rested my cheek against it for a moment.

"Will our baby come today, Mama?" I asked.

"I think maybe it will," she responded. "Hurry now, or you and Carol will be late!"

"Does Grandma have to come, Mama? I don't want her here!"

"Jennie! Don't you say such a thing! Grandma is going to help us while I go to the hospital. You be a good girl and help with your little sisters. And make sure you eat *everything* Grandma puts on your plate. You know how much that means to her."

Swallowing back a fresh wave of nausea, I left for school, wishing that I could be a real nurse and go to the hospital with Mother instead.

At recess, I told my friend Sarah that Grandma Gertrude was coming. Her response amazed me. "Oh, Jennie, you're so lucky," she said with envy. "I wish my grandma could come today. Nana Joy brings yummy treats in her purse and reads me stories."

Her comments left me even more depressed. We didn't have a nice name like Nana Joy to call our grandma. In fact, I secretly referred to our grandmother as Grandma No No, because the only "treat" she ever brought was canned peas, and she certainly never let us do anything fun.

A familiar car passed our bus with the driver honking and waving as we were riding home from school. Stopping at the next corner, our father got out and waved his arms for the bus to stop. I had never seen him so excited. "It's a *boy!*" he shouted. "*A boy!*" My sister Carol and I were allowed to leave the bus and ride the rest of the way home with our jubilant parent, who, after fathering four daughters, had been given a son that day.

When we got home, Grandma Gertrude actually *smiled* when Daddy excitedly told her the news, especially after hearing that the little boy would be called Ben, after her late husband and Daddy's father.

"There will *finally* be a boy to carry on the Afman family name," she said with satisfaction, and then she abruptly began dinner preparations. "Girls," she directed firmly, "set the table."

Carol laid out the plates and glasses, and I put the silverware at each place setting, my gaze drawn with dread to the counter where Grandma was working. A large can of peas stood at eye level on the counter, and I knew that Grandma No No and I would be at the table for an hour longer than any of the others. It was inevitable that once again we would be locked in a battle of wills until my plate was empty.

The next day when Daddy came home from the hospital, we talked.

"How come Grandma Gertrude is so mean?" I asked.

"Well, I don't believe *she* thinks she's being mean at all," Daddy replied.

"But she force-feeds me things I *hate*! She won't let me leave the table until the last bite is gone, and I swear she puts the biggest pile of vegetables on *my* plate!" I complained.

"Now, Jennie," he said, "*if* she does that, it's because she loves you and worries more about you since you were in the hospital with rheumatic fever. She wants to make sure you grow up strong and healthy."

"But it's not *fair!*" I wailed.

Daddy was quiet for a minute, his thoughts far away, and then he spoke.

"Jennie, did you know that your Grandpa Ben died when Grandma Gertrude was only forty-five years old? That may seem old to you, but it's awfully young to be left alone to raise four children."

"No." My father had never spoken of these things to me before. "How old were *you*, Daddy?"

"I was just sixteen." Sighing, he went on. "To be honest, your grandpa had a drinking problem, and he didn't always take care of our family very well." He looked me right in the eye. "Sometimes canned peas were all we had for supper, Jennie. Life has been both hard and sad for your grandma.

"Your mother gave birth to you and each of your sisters—and now your baby brother—in the hospital, and she has had the best care. Grandma Gertrude gave birth to eight babies at home, but only four of those babies survived. Her life has been very difficult."

Daddy chucked me under the chin and rose to go downstairs. "*Try* to be thankful for your grandma this week, okay?" he asked. "When you say your prayers tonight, will you ask God to help you to do that?"

The next day I looked at Grandma Gertrude differently. Her severe black dress was still the same, and she still walked with the same brisk sense of purpose, but I noticed other things about her. She was a determined woman who, in spite of great loss, never acted sorry for herself. She never wasted anything, and every action she took was for a reason. A seed of respect for my grandmother had taken root in my eight-year-old heart.

Many years have passed since that memorable week. Grandma Gertrude is in heaven now, along with both of her daughters. I like to think of her there—loving God and learning to laugh with abandon and to rest in his tender care. I realize now that I learned some important lessons from her: vegetables are good for you, work hard, avoid waste, and don't give up when life is difficult. I also learned that when I'm a grandmother myself someday, I should never, never, never come to visit my grandchildren bearing canned peas!

I hope she would be pleased that I am published using the name Jennie *Afman* Dimkoff and that I am carrying on the family name, in spite of being a woman. Most of all I am grateful that God reached down and removed the bitterness in a little girl's heart. I regret that I scrubbed off those obligatory kisses I gave my grandmother when I was young. Someday, I look forward to meeting my *new* Grandma Gertrude in heaven and running joyfully into her embrace.

Listen to your father, who gave you life, and do not despise your [grand]mother when she is old.

—PROVERBS 23:22 NIV

Does God love us because we are special—
or are we special because God loves us?[1]
—WILLIAM ARTHUR WARD

CHAPTER 19

Surprise at the Thrift Store

BY CAROL KENT

The women's retreat was taking place in a magnificent home in Virginia, and the back deck opened to a glorious view of the Appalachian Mountains. The surrounding sights and sounds sparkled with the unmistakable artistic touch of the creator.

Tanya was organizing this lovely event for the women in her church, and she longed for it to be a "marker weekend" in the lives of those who attended. In this exquisite setting, she wanted to give each woman something unique that would remind her of God's profound love for her—a keepsake that would bring back the memories of spending time alone with him far away from the clamor of everyday activities. Tanya's ministry budget was limited, so she needed to be resourceful.

She thought perhaps china teacups filled with inexpensive sentimental items hand-selected for the individual recipients would be within reach.

At home, money was tight and her husband's job as a policeman paid most of the bills, but Tanya's work as a nanny helped them to break even from month to month. They had finally purchased their own home, which was a great source of joy. Still, they were in the transition period of adjusting to new expenses that accompanied home ownership. There was no money for extras. However, Tanya felt blessed compared to the life she had known in her growing-up years. As a child she was abused and often went without adequate food and clothing. But instead of hardening her heart, the events of her past made her more compassionate toward the needs of others.

Unexpectedly, there was a change in direction for the family that employed her, and Tanya lost her job. She was thankful her children were home with her husband that day so she could freely weep over the lost income. Tanya explained: "Very much like the children of Israel walking from Egypt to the Promised Land, I doubted God again and again. Would he provide for me? Would he take care of my family? My life experience had not made it easy for me to trust and to rest in his provision."

When Tanya called her husband with the news, he was surprisingly optimistic and told her things would work out. He reminded her that God would take care of their needs. He was right, but at that moment despair was moving her spirits in a downward spiral.

On the way home she needed to pick up assorted china teacups at the local thrift shop for the women's retreat. She was praying for low-cost treasures, but her heart was heavy. As she walked in, not only did she find enough miscellaneous teacups for the upcoming conference in the mountains, but Tanya found herself in an aisle right next to an exquisite display of fine white china, trimmed with delicate yellow roses—a complete set of dinner plates, salad plates, bowls, cups, saucers, serving platters, and a gravy boat. Nothing was missing.

Tanya's mind swirled with random thoughts: *I've never had a set of fine china in my life! Yellow is my favorite color, and I love this pattern. But there's no price listed on the display, and I'm sure I can't afford it.*

Tanya and her husband were the youngest couple in their church. She loved her home and knew it was a gift from God, but it was modest and paled in comparison to the homes of the older women in their congregation. When they opened their homes for women's meetings, it was like walking into a *South-ern Living* magazine—stunning décor, fancy table settings, and sophisticated ambience.

For a moment she allowed her mind to dwell on the nega-tives: *I'm not a good cook. I love the Lord and enjoy having people in my home, but I don't have pretty things. My bathroom towels don't match—and neither do my dishes! Compared with others, I feel cheated, and sometimes I feel like a second-class citizen.* She knew she was grumbling—but somehow it fit the entire tone of her day.

Tanya stepped out of the store and called her husband. She told him about the china and how unbelievable it was that there was a full set at the thrift store. She forced a laugh, not wanting him to think she would be impractical enough to even think of purchasing something so frivolous. He paused and quietly said, "Go get the china."

"What?" Tanya said, still trying to shake the feelings of despair she had felt earlier.

He continued. "Go get the china, Tanya. Clearly your heav-enly father knows the desires of your heart, and you have waited for that china a long time. We will be okay financially. I don't want you to come home without the china."

Reluctantly, Tanya stepped back inside the store, knowing the cost would be prohibitive. She found a sales associate and asked how much they were asking for the lovely set of dinner-ware. The young clerk didn't know and eventually found the person who had authority over pricing.

Tanya looked up as a grandmotherly-looking woman moved in her direction with a rare combination of kindness and gusto. "Are you interested in the china, young lady?"

"Yes, I guess," Tanya responded hesitantly, "depending on the price."

"Well, let's come on over here and take a look." Tanya

obediently followed behind her like a child in tow, now feeling ridiculous for even asking about such expensive china. The clerk spoke slowly. "It's a nice set of dishes."

"Yes, ma'am," Tanya said, agreeing with her assessment. The woman looked at her for a moment, cocked her head, and smiled kindly as she said, "How does thirty dollars sound to you for the whole set?" Tears started making their way down Tanya's cheeks as she agreed to the ridiculously low price and helped to pack up her treasure.

As Tanya made her way home, a wave of thoughts mingled with her tears. *My daddy, my father in heaven, the only daddy I've ever known, wanted me to have a gift so special, so lovely, to make me know I'm loved and beautiful to him. He gave me an exquisite set of china on the day I lost my job, knowing that yellow roses are my favorite flowers. He wanted me to know I'm significant to him and that he knows the desires of my heart.*

Tanya was sure it would take at least two weeks to find another job as a nanny—but to her surprise, it took only two days! Later, she did an Internet search and discovered her china was called Royal Wentworth, and the replacement value was over $700. Tanya will never forget the day she lost her job and went searching for special teacups—and was amazed by God's yellow rose surprise.

————————

God can do anything, you know—far more than you could ever imagine or guess or request in your wildest dreams! He does it not by pushing us around but by working within us, his Spirit deeply and gently within us.

—EPHESIANS 3:20 MSG

————————

> Put your head on the chest of God and weep.[1]
> —NICOLE JOHNSON

CHAPTER 20

Beauty for Ashes

BY JENNIE AFMAN DIMKOFF

"Karen, get out!" Disoriented and crawling on the bedroom floor, Karen struggled to see through the thick smoke. "Just get out and get help! I'll get the girls," Willie yelled as he disappeared into the black fog, heading for their daughters' room.

Karen had tried to get them herself while her husband was downstairs checking on the extent of the fire, but the smoke had been too dense. They had no idea that the smoke from the fire had moved through a vent in the wall and directly into the girls' bedroom. Karen waited anxiously for Willie to emerge with the girls, but he did not. The seconds ticked by, and she felt rooted to the floor until finally, the realization struck her that the three people she loved most in the world were lost to her. The shock was so great that she just sat there while the flames licked higher and closer. She didn't know whether to stay and die with them or to try to leave.

An explosion below jarred her into action and she sprang to her feet. She had to get help! She tried to go downstairs, but her thoughts were disordered from the fumes. Could she save a photo album on this side of the house or try to reach the car keys? No. Everything was so hot it was dripping with fire, and things were exploding! Retreating to the master bedroom, she ran to the window. Miraculously, the week before, Willie had placed a ladder against the house—and it was resting beneath their window! After struggling to get the window open, Karen crawled over the sill, feeling for the ladder in the darkness. The heat of the fire was behind her, and in her desperation she had no thought of the freezing air that awaited her outside. She wore only long underwear and a pair of socks, and once she reached the bottom rung of the ladder she ran toward their neighbors, who lived a quarter of a mile down the country road. It was icy cold, wet, and dark. It was two thirty AM on Christmas morning.

A shocking sight awaited the neighbors when they were roused from their beds. In the glare of the porch light stood Karen Royster, freezing cold in soot-covered long johns and soaking-wet socks, with singed hair and burnt skin. She couldn't see very well, was gasping for breath, and was frantic with panic and grief. Emergency vehicles were called, and firefighters put out the blaze at the Royster home, which was declared a total loss. The body of William Royster was recovered holding both six-year-old Rachel and four-year-old Ruth in his arms. Karen was taken by ambulance to a hospital, where she spent four days and was treated for temporary blindness, smoke inhalation, and a burned lung.

Lying in her hospital bed, precious memories warred with the grief of stark reality. Christmas Eve had been so perfect. She and Willie had decided to start a new family tradition with the girls. Snuggling together on the couch, her handsome, loving husband had read them the Christmas story from the Bible. Then, rather than make the girls wait until Christmas morning, they had let them each open one present. It had been a precious family night, and at nine PM they had tenderly tucked their excited little daughters into bed. Then she and Willie had stayed up until midnight wrapping the rest of the gifts for their extended family, who would be coming for Christmas dinner the next day. It had been a joyful time. Willie had stoked the fire in the wood-burning stove before they went upstairs to bed.

The undertaker called on Karen while she was in the hospital to make the funeral arrangements. Utterly broken, she found some comfort when she learned that there was one casket large enough for all three to be buried in together. But while the medical staff could minister to Karen's physical needs, they could do nothing for her broken spirit. When the man left, she wept in desperation.

"God, everything is gone! All of my life has been wiped out from under me!" She no longer had her husband, her children, her home, or her possessions. There was no life insurance, and their home had been underinsured. At thirty-three years of age, she had *nothing*.

Lying there in utter desolation, Karen became aware of the presence of the Lord, and his quiet voice spoke to her very soul.

"You still have everything you need, Karen, because you still have me."

He reminded her of the story of Peter, who was able to walk on the water in the midst of a violent storm, as long as he kept his eyes on Jesus. There, in the hospital, a quiet peace came over her, and she clung to the assurance that as long as she kept her mind and heart on Jesus, she would somehow be carried through the painful storm that life had brought her way.

From her bed she wrote a beautiful letter to Willie and the girls that would be read at their funeral. It began with a love note to her husband, her hero, for loving her and for laying down his life trying to save their children, and it ended:

PS: Thank you, Jesus, that although I am now separated from my precious little girls, you have comforted me with knowing that Willie was holding Rachel and Ruth in his arms when they were ushered into heaven to see you face-

*to-face. I will hold your word near to my heart where in II
Samuel 1:23 it says, "In life they were loved and gracious,
and in death they were not parted."*

Karen was told that she had lost everything in the fire, but
as she clung to her faith like a lifeline, God touched her with
two blessings that would bring her great joy. Only two items
were salvaged from the devastating fire. The first was a photo
album, with precious photos of Willie, Ruth, and Rachel. Ruined on the outside, the photos inside were perfect, and they
were a priceless gift to Karen.

Second, a dear friend named Ray Carver showed up after
the fire and talked his way past the security line. Karen was a
classically trained violinist, and she had given lessons to Ray's
daughter. Carefully poking through the smoldering rubble,
he found what he was looking for. There in the ashes was
Karen's violin case. He hoped it held a treasure inside. It was
very hot; carefully removing it from the ruins, he made a call
to a restorer and asked what he should do. He was advised not
to open the case until it had cooled. When the case was finally
opened, Karen's priceless, handmade, two-hundred-year-old
Czechoslovakian violin was found inside with only one broken
string and slight water damage!

As Karen trusted God through the difficult weeks and
months ahead, he provided. A fund to help with funeral
expenses and her immediate needs was established through
the church, and a friend who wintered in Florida allowed
Karen to stay in her empty home. Grief-stricken and terribly
lonely, she spent time in God's Word and played her violin. In
those quiet times with the Lord, she discovered an unexpected
solace. She began to sing. With all of her formal musical training, she had never been a singer. And with the songs came joy
and peace.

Karen was still uncertain of the future, but friends offered to help her rebuild. Before a decision was made, a pastor friend invited her to come to a Sunday evening service at his church in Newaygo, Michigan, to play her violin, sing, and share her testimony for the first time since the tragedy.

That night, confirmed bachelor Al Brunsting sat in the audience as Karen sang, her beautiful face radiant with her love for the Lord. He leaned over to a friend and whispered, "I wish I could meet a girl like that." Then, as Karen haltingly shared her story, God touched Al's heart with a deep compassion and longing to know, help, and comfort Karen. Al was a businessman, but he also was a volunteer fireman, and because of that, he could understand Karen's experience better than many others.

Two weeks passed, and Al wrote Karen a letter asking if he could come and visit. With some trepidation, Karen said yes. He made the two-and-a-half-hour drive again the following week, and together they went to the gravesite of her family with flowers. It was little Rachel's birthday, and they grieved together. As weeks and months passed, a tender love blossomed.

On the fourth of July, they were married. Al laughingly jokes that he lost his independence on Independence Day, and together they faced a future that would include both joy-filled days and sudden bouts of deep sorrow as memories surfaced, but God had brought Al into Karen's life so she no longer had to face those sorrows alone. Shortly after their marriage, she became pregnant, and it soon became apparent that God was about to bless them abundantly! When she was eight months along, Al measured his tiny, five-foot-one wife's waistline, and it was four feet and one inch around! Just two weeks later, on the day before Mother's Day, their twins, Sarah and Seth, were brought into the world.

"We may never have all the answers to why things happen in life," says Karen, "but I believe that it is in times of deep distress that we see God's greatest display of love and faithfulness."

———————————

Thou hast turned for me my mourning into dancing: thou hast put off my sackcloth, and girded me with gladness.

—PSALM 30:11 KJV

———————————

> Your sister is your mirror, shining back
> at you with a world of possibilities.[1]
> —BARBARA ALPERT

CHAPTER 21

You Can't Tell Anyone!

BY CAROL KENT

Julie was pensive. *Every little girl should have a sister,* she thought. She had a brother who was two years her junior, but as long as Julie could remember, she had longed for a big sister, someone with whom she could share her clothes, her secrets, and her dreams. She often pretended that her aunt or her babysitter was her big sister. As time went on, she begged her mother to have another baby.

Her mother chuckled and said, "Julie, what if I had another baby and it turned out to be a boy?"

Julie put her hands on her hips and replied, "No! Absolutely not! I need a sister! Please, Mama."

Years went by and at age twenty-four, Julie was newly married and she and her mother worked for the same corporation. One afternoon her mother called and asked Julie if she could meet her outside where they could talk without interruptions. Julie vividly explained what happened next: "We stood on the bridge just outside the office and, lighting a cigarette, she calmly said, 'I have something to tell you.' My mother took another puff of her cigarette, exhaled slowly, and said, 'You have a sister.'"

Stunned, Julie looked at her mother with misgivings and reservation. *Is she out of her mind?* Julie's thoughts were reeling as she took in the unexpected and shocking announcement her mother had just made.

"How could that be possible?" Julie asked with hesitation.

Her mother immediately responded, "I was seventeen years old when I became pregnant." For several moments Julie was speechless, bewildered, and mystified by her mother's shocking revelation. Then her mother quickly added, "You can't tell anyone!"

• • •

When Julie's mother was growing up, having a child out of wedlock was reprehensible. She was the daughter of a proud Greek war veteran, and she knew she was a disgrace to her family. Julie later learned her mother ran away from home, managed to get a fake identification card, and found lodging and compassionate help at St. Vincent's, a Catholic home for unwed pregnant girls.

Over time, more details spilled out. The baby was born in November, and Julie's mother released her for adoption, while offering as little information as possible for the permanent birth record. She did, however, want the adoptive family to know the baby was already named Nanette.

During the next five years Julie was elated to think that somewhere in the world, she had a sister—a real "big sister"—but that thought was followed by the disappointment of realizing she would never know her. That didn't stop Julie from trying. She went on a quest to find Nanette with the minimal amount of information she had, but all of her attempts were futile.

• • •

Years ago in another suburb of Chicago, Nanette, age twelve, sat at the top of the staircase on an evening when her parents were entertaining company. Listening in on the adults' conversation, she learned that she had been adopted many years earlier. Nanette's parents kept her adoption a secret from most people. She was raised in the home of a wealthy doctor, but she suffered rejection from her adoptive mother and from her extended family members. Her brother was also adopted, and her mother made it known that he was the favorite child, causing Nanette loneliness and a feeling of isolation. As Nanette grew up, she longed to know where she came from. She wondered: *Who were my parents? Why was I released for adoption? Do I have any siblings?* Her search intensified as she longed to find a place of unconditional love and acceptance.

Nanette eventually discovered that her adoption was arranged through the Catholic Charities, and when she was in her early twenties, she began writing letters inquiring about her birth mother. Someone in the Charities' office responded kindly but told her the records were sealed and could not be released.

• • •

Five years passed, and it was the month of January. Julie was six months pregnant with her first child. The phone rang. It was her mother, but her voice sounded strained, as if something was wrong. Julie asked her what was troubling her, and her mother answered, "No, no, nothing's wrong." Julie persisted, and finally her mother relented. "I received a letter today."

Instinctively Julie recognized the cause of her mother's angst and she blurted out, "It was from St. Vincent's, wasn't it?"

Her mother was incredulous. "How did you know?" *How did I know? I felt in my heart that I was about to hear information I have wanted to know all of my life!*

With excitement building, Julie asked her mother what the letter said. Her mother's immediate response was "You can't tell anyone!" Julie felt frustrated, but she knew her mother was overwhelmed by the news she had just received. Her mom continued. "Well, your sister wants to meet me."

Julie was exuberant and she could hardly contain her emotions. "Mom, this is awesome! I've longed for a sister ever since I can remember—and she wants to meet you? I hope that means I'll get to meet her too!"

Julie's mother soberly said, "I'm not sure about all of this, and I don't know what I should do." It soon became apparent that her mom was worried about how the family would respond. She was anxious about telling her parents, her son, and other relatives. This secret had been kept for a long time. However, Julie was so thrilled she couldn't see a downside. She had a sister who wanted to meet her family! Julie talked to her mom a while longer and encouraged her to take the risk.

A few days later, Julie's mom agreed to meet Nanette. The woman at the adoption agency was extremely helpful, and arrangements were made for the reunion to take place in a local restaurant in Darien, Illinois. Julie's mom and dad arrived early and sat down, nervously awaiting Nanette's arrival.

A beautiful young woman walked into the restaurant. Nanette's dad spotted her first. His eyes welled up with tears as he said, "Oh my, it's Julie!" No, it was Nanette, but she looked so much like Julie that the resemblance was astounding.

Following warm greetings and hugs, there were lots of questions. Nanette learned that her biological mother and father married each other not long after she was adopted, because they were in love and her mom was pregnant again—this time with Julie. By then her mother had turned eighteen years old. Nanette was speechless as her father told of getting "the beating of his life" from his own dad when he found out about the pregnancy.

Nanette was overwhelmed by the news that her mother and father remained together, married, and had two more children. Tears flowed as Nanette discovered that two years after Julie was born, Peter arrived. She had a sister and a brother she never knew about.

A few weeks later the entire family met for dinner. Nanette walked into the house, and there were joyful introductions all around. For a moment, time stood still as Nanette and Julie took a good look at each other. It was like gazing into a mirror. Their dark brunette hair was identical in color and style. Their facial features were so similar they could have been twins. Julie's heart almost leaped out of her chest as she thought, *Finally, I really have a sister!* They loved each other instantly.

• • •

It has been sixteen years since that reunion, and Julie and Nanette have become close. Through good times and tough times, they have found comfort, support, encouragement, and joy in their growing relationship. God knew the longing of their hearts and his blessing came through a mirror image when he brought two sisters into each other's lives. They missed the companionship of their childhood, but they have the rest of their lives to build new memories.

All my longings lie open before you, O Lord;
my sighing is not hidden from you.

—PSALM 38:9 NIV

The reason we go to church is not because we have our lives together, but because our lives are broken. It is a hospital for people who are hurting and need healing and wholeness.
—REVEREND CASE ADMIRAAL

CHAPTER 22

The Church That Practiced
What It Preached

BY JENNIE AFMAN DIMKOFF

Sitting in the family pew, clutching her keys, and ready to bolt, Maurene's tears started to roll as the pastor stepped up to the pulpit with the letter in his hand. Her kids were with her, but her husband Jim was on a business trip. Maurene felt frightened, exposed—and ashamed.

Addressed to the congregation, it was a letter of apology from Maurene herself. After years as a faithful office manager, she had embezzled funds from the physicians she worked for. The next day she was going to court to be sentenced. There was the desperate hope that she would be put on probation, but deep down, she and her husband knew better. She would be sent to a federal prison.

She and Jim had decided that it would be better to be upfront with their church family rather than let them hear the news from rumors, or worse yet, the newspaper or television. The fact that they were volunteer leaders made the confession all the more painful. As Maurene sat there with the pastor reading the damning words of her confession and contrite apology, her six-year-old daughter sat beside her on one side and her nine-year-old son on the other. Putting her arms around them, she hung her head in shame and waited for the stones to fly.

Maurene felt a hand on her shoulder. Looking back, she

saw her friend Kristi in the pew behind her, gently offering what she had least expected—love and support. There were tears in Kristi's eyes, and Maurene started sobbing as the pastor continued reading.

Maurene's letter was not only a confession and an apology, but also a request that the church not hold her mistakes against her family. Instead, she asked the church to help care for them while she was away paying the price for her sin. Amazingly, arms reached out from everywhere, and rather than running from the church that morning, it took Maurene over an hour to leave because so many people wanted to encourage her in some way!

Driving home, she praised God for leading them to that wonderful church twelve years before. She realized there were other things to be grateful for as well. The day that had started out so miserably had become a day of hope and an opportunity to count her blessings. She could hardly wait for Jim to get home that night so she could tell him what had happened. Would God work in the heart of the judge tomorrow as well?

• • •

Although Sunday had been a blessing, the reality of Monday and the dread that accompanied it was inescapable. Maurene and Jim drove to the courthouse at the state capitol an hour away for her sentencing. Her heart thundered as they approached the courtroom. However, when they arrived, there stood the pastor, another friend from church, and several family members filling a whole row in the courtroom!

When the physicians arrived, they sat directly behind Maurene. The facts of the case were presented, and Maurene hung her head in shame, knowing her family, pastor, friend, and employers who had trusted her were hearing the details of her crime.

When the judge was ready to pronounce the sentence,

Maurene was asked to stand. Addressing her formally, the judge said a number of things, but a few statements stuck out most to Maurene: "You have committed a serious crime and must be punished. However, I am impressed with the support system you have in place, and I can tell that both you and your family are going to survive this experience. I sincerely wish you well, and I hope that you use the time while you are away to get your life in order, so that you can come home to your wonderful family.

"You are hereby sentenced to eighteen months in a federal prison."

Dread and relief comingled at that moment. Maurene wasn't thrilled to hear that she would be going away for a year and a half, but her attorney had warned her that she could receive up to *ten years,* so she considered herself fortunate. Instead, she had received the minimum sentence. Following the hearing, he explained that there was no federal prison in their home state of Michigan, and he thought Maurene would be sent to a facility in Illinois or Ohio because the court usually kept prisoners within five hundred miles of home.

"You'll get a notice from the court to self-surrender in about six weeks," he said. "Get your affairs in order now, before you have to leave your family." Maurene was thankful for the timing, because it meant she would be home for their son's birthday and would be able to get the children back in school before leaving. However, just fourteen days after her sentencing, she received a letter instructing her to self-surrender to Alderson Federal Prison Camp in West Virginia, which was more than seven hundred fifty miles away, in just two weeks!

That night, Maurene had the difficult task of telling her children she would be going far away.

Climbing into her mother's lap, six-year-old little Mackenzie asked, "Why did you take all that money, Mommy?"

Maurene swallowed hard. "I thought that I needed the stuff that the money could buy."

Innocent eyes looked intently into her mother's, and Mackenzie responded, "But, Mom, you know *stuff* doesn't mean anything."

"I know that now, honey," Maurene said with tears stinging her eyes. She hugged her child tightly. "I know that now."

The next fourteen days were chaotic. With huge debt hanging over their heads, Maurene and Jim had already filed for bankruptcy and their house had gone into foreclosure. Knowing that Jim would be left to deal with everything alone, Maurene desperately wanted to get her family settled before she had to leave. She found a house to rent, but it was twenty miles away from all they found familiar, which saddened her greatly.

Two days before she was to report to Alderson, Maurene was unpacking at the rental house, trying to get her family settled before she left. Jim had said his good-byes, as he had a trip to Colorado already scheduled prior to learning when she would have to leave, and they needed every penny of his income as a long-distance bus driver. He had taken their son with him, so that was one less painful good-bye she would deal with. Mackenzie would stay with Maurene's mother until Jim returned. It was hot, and there was no air-conditioning as she and her daughter unpacked boxes. Maurene committed as much to memory as she could so she would be able to picture her family living there in the old farmhouse.

Hearing a car door slam, Maurene went to the door and recognized a woman from church. Their kids were in the same classes at school so they had seen each other, but that was about it. Her name was Amy Winters.

"Hi, Maurene," Amy called, walking up the drive with a card in her hand. "I believe God laid it on my heart to come and tell you that I'll take care of your family while you're gone." She had tears in her eyes. "Give our number to Jim so we can work out a schedule for when he has to go out of town. Mike and I will care for your kids and make sure they have whatever they need."

Maurene was in tears before Amy left because a heavy burden was lifted from her shoulders. Without doubt, God had touched them that day with the blessing of Amy, and her offer wasn't just talk. It was genuine.

Two of Maurene's siblings and a niece drove her to West Virginia, where she was "processed in" at Alderson Federal Prison Camp to begin life as an inmate. While there, she spent a lot of time in God's Word, enabled by the women in her church Bible study group, who sent her their notes each week. Another woman made sure she received her pastor's sermon on tape weekly.

The guards at the prison treated her humanely, although once she got caught talking when it wasn't allowed and was disciplined. She had to push the "Cadillac," which was the name they gave the broom. But even that was good, because the other inmates realized Maurene was just like them and started to trust her more. She was given a job she loved as a teacher's aide, helping inmates get their GEDs.

Although far from home, she received a letter from someone at church every single day. Maurene figured that would end after a while, but it didn't. When her family was financially strapped without her income, she was shocked and humbled to receive the news that a couple from their church was paying their rent while she was away! Their neighbors Amy and Mike took in their children as if they were their own, making sure they had school supplies, clothes, and even cupcakes for class parties. Maurene's husband would not have been able to keep his job, which often took him out of town, had it not been for them. Repeatedly, God showed love and grace for Maurene and her family through individuals in their congregation.

Maurene did a lot of soul-searching while an inmate and left Alderson a better person. Not only was she finally rid of the guilt that had pulled her down, but she also knew for certain that she was forgiven by God and that there was still a place for her in heaven. She also loved her husband Jim more than ever. Through all that had happened, he had never uttered a bad word about what she had done or how it had affected him and the kids. He still loved her dearly.

Amazingly, a former employer had a job waiting for her upon her release from prison. And one of the greatest blessings for Maurene was to be able to return to her church and be welcomed with open arms, never feeling that she should stay in the background. She got right back into serving joyfully—singing in the choir, working with women's ministries, and later becoming the Sunday School superintendent.

Redeem means a number of things, including "to win back," "to free from what distresses or harms," "to reform," and "to restore." Maurene experienced God's blessing of sweet redemption not only through his forgiveness of her sin but also by the hand of her church family. The director of women's ministries who worked side by side with Maurene during the years that followed made this comment: "We've all moved beyond this. I believe our pastor set the tone for forgiveness and love to be shown. There was no need for shame or guilt. Jesus had already borne that at the cross."

Make this your common practice. Confess your sins
to each other and pray for each other so that you
can live together whole and healed.

—JAMES 5:16A MSG

Purpose in life is not just something we do. It involves who we are and our way of being in this world.[1]

—JAN JOHNSON

CHAPTER 23

Formula for Life

BY CAROL KENT

The excitement of Christmas was over. The year turned the corner into 1979 and winter began. For Mary Kay Roy, January was usually a time to catch up after the busy holiday season and to regroup before plunging into new activities—but this year was different.

She was launching a class at her church. Her days had been spent studying, planning, and praying about this new opportunity. The Bible had been an important, life-changing tool in her own life, and she wanted to share it with others. Because the class preparation and the mentoring that came with it claimed much of her time and attention, she was slow to notice the change in her husband's demeanor. However, she soon noticed discouragement in Shane's eyes, along with dissatisfaction with his work. Since he was by nature a quiet man, she had not observed the beginning of this significant change.

Shane was forty-three, a pediatric nephrologist (kidney disease specialist), an associate professor with the University of Tennessee, Memphis, and head of his section. His work was definitely not boring or monotonous; it was varied and interesting. He taught medical students, residents, and fellows; he had a limited private practice, did clinical research, and was codirector of the Pediatric Dialysis Unit. But all the joy and enthusiasm for his work had disappeared. For weeks Mary Kay watched him leave for work as tired and weary as a person might be coming home after a stressful day. He occasionally mentioned problems at work, personal discouragement, and his feeling of going nowhere.

Shane and Mary Kay did not talk about this situation often. Talking did not seem to help or change anything. Because of his personality and dependability, he continued to do his work, but with a sense of resignation. Outwardly he looked the same, but inwardly there was uneasiness and quiet desperation. After twenty-three years of marriage, Mary Kay knew what her mate was feeling. He was in such distress that she, too, was suffering. Her heart ached for a way to lift his depression, but none of her efforts impacted his malaise.

In May, a friend recommended the book *Men in Midlife Crisis* by Jim Conway. This book helped Mary Kay understand the frustrations and pressures men experience in the workplace, their enormous sense of responsibility to provide for their families, and the realization that they only have a limited number of years to be promoted before society begins looking toward younger men. Learning about these issues helped Mary Kay understand Shane, but it did not change anything.

Mary Kay wondered how she could help her spouse—this man she loved so much that when he hurt, she hurt. She made every effort to keep domestic problems from being his burden. She made sure their home was a place of refuge and lightheartedness. But she soon discovered that cheerfulness around a depressed person seems to have the opposite effect.

In desperation she acknowledged her helplessness and frustration to God. Something needed to change. Instead of telling God how to answer her prayers, as she'd done in the past, she asked him to restore Shane's joy and enthusiasm in his work. Much later, Mary Kay said, "I am grateful I left the details in God's hands, because I could never have imagined the astonishing remedy he provided."

• • •

Late in June, God began to answer not only Mary Kay's prayer, but also the prayers of several parents who were watching their babies starve with an unknown illness. The hospital where Shane worked admitted two babies with a similar medical puzzle. The babies were not growing, even though they were taking in enough formula. Blood tests suggested an inherited kidney disease. Although Shane's research was clinical and not done in the laboratory, he had the same searching nature as the people who did lab research.

Shane and one of his partners began to take steps to solve this malnutrition mystery. They checked literature that listed the ingredients in the formula. It was supposed to include sufficient ingredients for growth, but the minerals deficient in the babies' blood tests were also deficient in the formula. Adding the missing ingredients to the formula made a notable improvement and ruled out inherited disease.

On July 22, 1979, the hospital admitted a third baby with similar symptoms. Shane immediately asked, "What formula is the baby taking?"

"The same as the other two babies" was the reply. The formula manufacturer was consulted and asked if any similar cases had been reported. The answer was no—until thirty-six hours after Shane's initial call.

Shane had the formula tested by two laboratories, and the mystery was solved. The formula did not contain what its label claimed. By then, the hospital authorities, local health authorities, and the Centers for Disease Control had been alerted. Meetings were held with the manufacturer, multiple doctors, and health organizations. The formula was recalled from the market. As swift actions were taken to remedy the problem, Shane was excited. He talked about what had happened with doctors across the country, as well as with those in his own hospital. The phones never stopped ringing.

One day Mary Kay realized Shane was so engrossed in trying to find the solution to this problem that his depression had dissipated. God had answered her prayer in a way she never could have imagined. She thought, *Dare I tell Shane about my prayer?* She watched his enthusiasm and excitement grow as he realized the research possibilities of this experience.

One night as they were getting ready for bed, she had just finished brushing her teeth and Shane was setting the alarm for the morning. She marveled, realizing a new day was something he now looked forward to with anticipation. Still holding her toothbrush, Mary Kay stepped into the bedroom and said, "There is something I need to tell you." Shane looked at her expectantly. After a deep breath she said, "I asked God to do something to restore your joy and enthusiasm for work, but I never dreamed he would answer this big."

Shane fell back on the bed with a thud—like he had been hit in the pit of his stomach. He suddenly realized God had been in control of this entire process and the thought was astounding—not only that God had revealed the answer to this "failure to thrive" problem for the babies, but that God had used Shane as a major point person in the process, in direct answer to his wife's prayers.

This discovery and subsequent television coverage led to a representative from the state of Tennessee holding a congressional hearing on recalls and controls on the composition of infant formula. This and additional hearings culminated in the writing and passing of the Infant Formula Act, which was signed into law by President Jimmy Carter on September 26, 1980. Shane was privileged to attend the signing of this bill.

That year God blessed Mary Kay's husband with a sense of purpose that put meaning and fulfillment back into his life.

Shane knew his work was important and that the lives of children were saved as a result of his research.

Mary Kay's gifted and humble husband went home to be with the Lord last year, but she will never forget how God answered her prayer for her spouse in a life-altering and spectacular way.

The Lord says, "I will guide you along the best pathway for your life. I will advise you and watch over you."

—PSALM 32:8 NLT

I believe that God is in the miracle business—that His favorite way of working is to pick up where our human abilities and understandings leave off and then do something so wondrous and unexpected that there's no doubt who the God is around here.[1]

—EMILIE BARNES

CHAPTER 24

House for Sale

BY JENNIE AFMAN DIMKOFF

"I wish I could go with you this morning."

"Me, too, dear, but you can pray from here. I'm counting on that." Dad bent and kissed Mom good-bye and headed for the door.

"Tell Madelyn I said hello if you have time to see her this afternoon!" she called after him, and then sighed, leaning back against the cushioned rocker. My mother, Pauline Afman, was recovering from a heart condition, and it was discouraging for her to still feel as weak as a kitten.

When I was a freshman in high school, our family moved from Durand to Sandusky, Michigan, where my father became the pastor of a local church. That morning Dad was making the long drive to the burn clinic in Ann Arbor. We were planning to visit a man from our church who had been severely burned in an oil pit fire at the auto maintenance business where he worked. If there was time after visiting with the patient and his family, Dad hoped to be able to stop in Durand on his way back to check on the condition of our old house there. He and Mama owned the home, and our family had lived there during his former pastorate. The church in Durand had rented it for a few months following our move but had decided to buy a parsonage, and the home was now empty. My parents immediately put the home up for sale and ran ads in the paper, with no response. The empty home, so many miles away, was a financial burden to them, and they *needed* to find a buyer.

Closing her eyes, Mama thought about her handsome husband and all the heaviness that was on his mind and heart that day. With hands folded in her lap, she turned her heart toward her heavenly father and prayed. "Bless the Lord, O my soul, and all that is within me, bless his holy name."

Words of praise came easily to her lips, and after a few minutes, Mama moved on to lay her concerns before the Lord: the burn victim and his family, her husband as he traveled and met with them, and the empty house in Durand that they needed to sell but felt so helpless to manage from such a distance. Peace washed over her as she prayed, and once again she found herself thanking the Lord for his faithfulness to them.

Hours later, my dad, Pastor Clyde Afman, left the hospital complex in Ann Arbor and headed toward Durand, Michigan. His heart was still heavy for his parishioner and his family. The man had been badly burned but would recover. He had spent time in prayer with the family and had rejoiced with them when they finally heard good news from the doctor. Still, it would be a long recovery.

He didn't have a key to the house in Durand and needed to get off at the Linden Lake exit and stop and pick it up from their friend Madelyn Menzel, a retired real estate broker who had volunteered to show the house if anyone was interested. Tired and so preoccupied with thoughts of the burn victim, Dad passed the exit without even realizing it. The next exit was miles ahead, and he was dismayed, realizing the time he would be wasting. It dawned on him that he should stop and phone Madelyn and make sure she was home. Since he hadn't known if or when he would be able to leave the hospital, he hadn't contacted her earlier. If she wasn't even there, it would be even more of a waste of time to turn around and drive back.

It was the sixties, long before cell phones, and as Dad pulled off at the next exit, he scanned the area for a gas station with a phone booth out front. Sure enough, there was a booth, but to his frustration, a car was parked nearby and a man was in the booth using the phone. Dad pulled up behind the other vehicle and waited . . . and waited. The man seemed to be taking forever.

Tired and a bit irritated, my father figured that if he got out of his car and stood beside the phone booth, the fellow would get the idea that someone else needed to make a call. As he approached the booth, he noticed that the man had a newspaper open in front of him and that he seemed to be searching through the want ads. Was he looking for a job? Could he possibly be looking for a home to buy? As my dad waited, he started to pray.

When the man finally emerged from the booth, Dad approached with a smile.

"Hello there. I hope my standing here didn't rush you too much."

The man mumbled an apology for taking so long and waved the want ads rather helplessly.

"I couldn't help but notice that you were studying some ads. Could I inquire if you were by any chance looking to buy a house?" Dad asked. "Because my wife and I just happen to have a home in Durand that is for sale."

Looking up in surprise, the man said that indeed he was and that the Durand area was *exactly* where he and his wife were looking to buy! Dad thrust out his hand and introduced himself to the fellow, whose name was Mr. Zager, and set up an appointment to show the home to him and his wife the following week.

Within a minute after my dad waved good-bye to Mr. Zager, Mama answered our phone at home in Sandusky and heard his excited voice on the other end of the line.

"Pauline, you won't believe it! I'm so excited I couldn't wait until I got home to tell you what happened!"

Standing in the very phone booth he had waited so impatiently to use, Dad told Mama the amazing story about missing the Linden Lake exit and meeting the potential buyer of their home.

The man God had waiting in the phone booth did indeed buy their house, and Pastor Clyde and Pauline Afman would never forget how God blessed their lives that day. What my Dad had thought was a wrong exit, an inconvenience, and a waste of his time was actually a miraculous gift from God—an answer to both of their prayers.

Bless the Lord, O my soul:
And all that is within me, bless his holy name!

—PSALM 103:1 NKJV

If I dare to live the authentic life I was created to live, it will be messy at times, not always tidy. But if I don't live authentically, I run the risk of losing my zest for life. As I abide in Christ, all of life becomes more sacred, and I become more Real.[1]

—BRENDA WAGGONER

CHAPTER 25

The Timing of Fireworks

BY CAROL KENT

"I gotta go, Allison, I think I'm on the wrong road!" April's eagerness to share her transformation with her spiritual confidante would have to wait. As the call ended, she assessed her situation. *I'm in the dark, lost, and alone.*

After a hasty exit and a U-turn, she let out a sigh of relief. Finding her way onto I-77 South, she geared up for the long, ten-hour drive home. Suddenly she heard loud, frightening sounds. *Boom!* Followed by *crack! Sizzle! Pop!* She covered her head and gripped the steering wheel. April's white knuckles seemed to melt into hues of red, blue, and green as she hung on for dear life.

Out of nowhere fireworks filled the sky. Her thoughts swirled: *But it isn't even the Fourth of July! Where are these fireworks coming from?* The brilliance was overwhelming and she wanted to pull over and enjoy the spectacle, but she was far from home so she kept driving. As she pulled out from under the canopy of light and sound, she involuntarily recited the last quote she heard at the seminar she had attended on the weekend: "When your joy in me, meets my joy in you, there are *fireworks* of heavenly ecstasy."[2] At that moment, April knew she was on the right road.

Joy could not even begin to describe what she was feeling! The discovery April made on her journey had actually started seven years earlier. For all those years she had actively guarded herself from sharing the secrets of her past: how her father had murdered his wife and committed suicide in front of her three young siblings and her failed attempt to adopt her step-brothers.

Her mind raced: *I can share about my military upbringing, my tormented graduate school years, and the loss of our first two children in miscarriages, but I can't share what happened to my dad!*

April and her younger brother, Michael, were "army brats." As children of a retired United States Army first sergeant, they had certain standards to uphold: *Be in control at all times. Never disgrace your family, your country, or yourself. Family matters are not shared around the base and certainly not in public.*

After ten years of retirement, getting married again, and becoming a new father, her dad still exuded his military bearing. However, he broke this code of conduct when he took his wife's life and then committed suicide, forever changing April's future.

On Thursday, August 1, 2002, at 11:17 PM, April's world turned upside down. After she reeled from the shocking news, questions swirled in her mind: *Why wasn't I notified of my father's or stepmother's deaths for eight hours? Why didn't the law enforcement officers provide information about my half brothers' whereabouts? Why did the state police require supervised visitation the first time I saw them? Why was it difficult to speak to my step-mother's family? Why were my husband and I not awarded custody of my three half brothers? Was it because I was the daughter of the murderer?*

The only thing April could say to her stepmother's family was "I'm so sorry." In the months following the loss of her dad and stepmother, it was "guilt by association" that explained why only a small handful of sympathy cards arrived, and even fewer people phoned to voice any compassion for her loss. April avoided shopping in stores when she was home for the holidays to avoid chatting with old friends. Returning to work after two weeks, she simply said, "My father and stepmother died tragically." She didn't purposefully hide what her father did, but she was afraid. Fear of judgment and public condemnation crippled April from the inside out.

They lived a five-hour drive from the scene of the crime. April's husband Jason was a respected up-and-coming assistant principal, and April was the college counselor at a prestigious boarding school. People trusted them with their children! She wondered: *If people knew I was the daughter of a murderer, would they want us working with their kids? Would they want us to work in our church ministries?*

April's upbringing had preconditioned her to keep silent about the story. Few people reached out, and when they did, her military upbringing dictated that she politely decline their sympathy. She lost herself in pride, shame, and fear. Terrified that people would judge her based on her father's wrongful actions, she simply decided she would never speak about it. Praying, she spoke aloud: "God, I am grateful for my gifts to speak, share, and encourage, and I'll use them, but don't make me talk about my father." But April had discovered that barricading herself behind her own secrets was a prison of her own making, and it was definitely not God's plan for a productive future.

Later that night, somewhere near the Ohio and West Virginia border, she made another call. "Georgie Anne, the speaking seminar in Michigan was transformational. I finally shared my testimony about my dad! I feel free and liberated! God blessed me in a mighty way, but I am so exhausted. I don't think I can make it all the way back to Virginia tonight. I'd like to stay overnight in your area and go to church with you in the morning." With great Southern hospitality, Georgie Anne warmly welcomed April, rejoiced over her news, and then followed up with directions to a nearby hotel and worship times for services the following day.

Georgie Anne called back within minutes. "April, after we hung up, I grabbed my church bulletin. Right now we don't have a pastor, and I just realized the guest speaker tomorrow might be someone you know." The next words out of Georgie Anne's mouth shocked April. "It's Pastor John King. Do you know him?"

April's mind whirled. It felt like she stepped on the brake, skidded over onto the shoulder of the road, plowed into the grass, and came to a complete stop. *Do I know him?* she thought. *Yes, I know him! He was my pastor my last year of high school. John King knew my dad. He went to school with my dad; they were friends. I attended church camp with his daughter. We have a history with each other, and he knows our family's secret.*

For the next hour and a half of her drive, April prayed. *God, are you serious? You and I did some amazing work this past week at the conference in Michigan. It was a true breakthrough for me! I did what you wanted. I shared my most painful story out loud—in front of other people! This is too fast for me. I can't be vulnerable in front of Pastor King.*

April tangibly felt God's joy at that very moment, but she was also filled with apprehension. Her old friends pride, guilt, and shame found familiar seats in her car. They buckled themselves in as if to say, "We have no plans to leave, April. Being authentic and vulnerable will only bring you pain. Stay comfortable with your secret. Don't talk about your painful past. It's too risky."

Resisting former patterns, April slipped off her shoes and declared each mile of her remaining drive to the hotel to be "holy ground." April experienced a myriad of emotions: "Through tears, moments of yelling, and confession, I knew God was not just calling me to speak out loud but to *live* out loud." Checking into her hotel room, April fell on her face before the Lord. It was two AM. She didn't even open the bed-sheets or change her clothes. She knew the next day would require speaking to Pastor King, facing her past, and living authentically. She wanted to be spiritually prepared.

When morning dawned, April knelt in prayer. She could not remember the entire passage in Ephesians 6 that lists the armor of God, but she knew she needed to be ready to fight an emotional and spiritual battle. Her mind raced. *I have a three-year-old who wears his sword and shield to the grocery store. I should know that scripture! What is that last piece of armor?* She prayed: *Father God, I can't even remember what piece I am missing, but will you help me to put on the whole armor of God?*

Moments later these words came: *I desire truth in your in-ward parts.*

TRUTH! The belt of truth! Satisfied, she finally understood that it wasn't just a verbal listing of armor that would prepare her for the day ahead. God spoke to her spirit and said, *April, my truth will help you to live authentically.*

Driving to the church, she knew this day was not about meeting Pastor King. April was facing her own sin of shame, guilt, pride, and fear. It had been a long ride and April was longing for the freedom that comes when we are honest about our past and find joy in facing the truth. She knew this journey would be a complete transformation from the inside out. It required courage, boldness, and endurance. The hardest part was taking the first step.

God did not send fireworks that morning, but once at the church, April's eyes landed above the fireplace in the foyer. Engraved there were these words: *I am the Way, the Truth, and Life. No one comes to the Father except through me.*

April found comfort in those words, but her thoughts played tug-of-war: *God, will Pastor King remember me? What does*

he think of me and of my family? I know he ministered to the family
of the victims of my father's crime, and he knows I'm the daughter
of the murderer. I know I have to face him, but I'm afraid.

"Through you, Lord, here I come," April whispered, walking into the sanctuary. After the service she found herself making a mad dash to Pastor King, reminding him of who she was.
Words tumbled out quickly as she told of the powerful way
God was transforming her life.

His response was kind and compassionate. "April, I am so
happy to hear how God is working in your life." Her guilt over
what her father had done more than seven years before began
diminishing as she received acceptance and genuine compassion from Pastor King. She then looked for Pastor King's wife.

Working her way through the crowd, she hesitantly approached Mrs. King. Before long she found herself in the arms
of a caring friend, not a judgmental critic, as she shared her
heart with someone who knew the pain of her past. "April, you
are pure. You are clean." It was as if Mrs. King understood that
she had felt guilty by association, and she and her husband had
both discerned that April needed to know others did not see
her in a negative light. Mrs. King's kind words were another
reminder that she was not responsible for her father's sin.

A spark of joy began to fill April's heart as she realized she
could be honest about her family's past. Instead of living in
the dread of having the truth revealed, she was free to begin
sharing her own story in appropriate ways. That day God surprised April again as she looked up in the sky and gazed upon
a fully arched rainbow. She sensed God's pleasure and felt like
the heavens were proclaiming, "Welcome back to Virginia!"

April arrived home in time to tuck her young son into bed.
He was her small knight in shining armor. It felt good to be
home again, and the joy she felt earlier now permeated every
part of her heart and soul.

That night she prayed, *Lord, I've been a mess for seven years—in bondage to my family's devastating past history. I know you are calling me to be vulnerable and authentic. Thank you for healing my broken heart and giving me the privilege of helping others who have come from difficult beginnings. You are healing me on the inside, and I sense your acceptance, delight, and blessing. I want to reflect your joy by the way I live my life. I want to find my deepest delight in knowing you.*

Four months later, on a different road and in the company of her husband and brother, joy converged again. Healing was taking place in the hearts of her extended family members too. As they shared their stories, other people were finding renewed hope and fresh faith.

Suddenly, April's husband spoke up as he pointed across the dashboard. "Look over there. Did you see that?"

"No, what was it?" April asked.

"Fireworks!" he said with an enthusiastic tone.

April had to admit she didn't actually *see* them, but she smiled, knowing she was experiencing an explosion of new joy in her life. What perfect timing! She was living in the smile of God's approval. He had touched her life with authenticity and she felt his pleasure.

Behold, you delight in truth in the inward being,
and you teach me wisdom in the secret heart.

—PSALM 51:6 ESV

I remember my mother's prayers, and they have always followed me. They have clung to me all my life.[1]
—ABRAHAM LINCOLN

CHAPTER 26

New Shoes for Amber

BY JENNIE AFMAN DIMKOFF

My husband and I were married for nine years before we had our first child, and when Amber Joy came into our lives with her dark, silky hair and big, brown eyes, Graydon and I were *sure* that no other baby on earth had ever been more perfect. We had been childless for so long, it seemed that everyone we knew showered us with gifts. I loved choosing from an array of little garments, wrapping Amber in handmade blankets crocheted by dear friends, and I especially enjoyed the tiny little shoes that lined a shelf in her closet.

I would often stand holding Amber against my shoulder in front of the mirror and watch her reflection as she slept. I'd nestle the softness of her head in my neck and think to myself, *I want to engrave this picture in my heart forever. I never want to forget how precious my baby is or how it looks and feels to hold her like this.*

Each advance was recorded in her baby book: the first smile, laughter, and giggle. Amber crawled backward at seven months and forward at eight. Graydon and I cheered her on like an Olympian! At nine months she crawled up the stairs after our cat, and that same month she stood alone. Once she "found" her legs at ten months, she was determined to stay standing and mobile—but she fell a lot. As the months went by and she continued to stumble, I didn't give it much thought, chalking up her clumsiness to the thickness of the diapers between her little legs.

After a Sunday service, my friend Phyl, who helped in the nursery that morning, took me aside when I arrived to pick up Amber.

"Jennie, when is your next appointment with Amber's pediatrician?" she asked cautiously.

"Not for a while. She had her one-year checkup in August and she's doing great!" I responded enthusiastically, but a tremor of uneasiness went through me. It was the first week of November. "Why do you ask?"

Phyl sighed. "She's having trouble walking, Jennie. Compared to the other children her age, she can't walk nearly as far without falling. I think you should make an appointment."

My eyes locked with those of my friend, and I nodded while dread filled my being. Amber, in the meantime, pulled herself up against a toy box, smiled broadly, and after two awkward steps, fell solidly on her diapered bottom.

The following day I made an appointment with our doctor, who sent us on to an orthopedist. In laymen's terms, we were told that Amber's legs had an abnormal curvature from the knee to the ankle. We were given two options. The bones could be broken and straightened surgically, or we could try something that would take much longer. She could be fitted with a twister cable. It had a wide, reinforced belt that attached around the waist with black cables that strapped onto the outside of the legs and attached to child-sized orthopedic shoes.

The idea of breaking Amber's legs horrified us. "How long would she have to wear the cables?" I asked.

"Twenty-two hours a day for at least four years," the doctor explained. "We may be able to have her out of them in time to start kindergarten."

Four days before Christmas, Amber Joy was fitted with little orthopedic shoes that were permanently attached to the cable contraption, and for twenty-two hours a day we put up with it. She adjusted far more easily than I did. That ugly thing had to be worn over every pretty little outfit I dressed her in, and, worse than that, it made my beautiful child look *disabled*. And for another thing, I *really* missed the cute shoes. She wore that one scuffed pair of orthopedic shoes with *everything*. It was impossible to keep them looking new and shiny. I hated them!

Then one day I had a wake-up call. A dear friend miscarried for the second time, and her grief was overwhelming. Suddenly, I saw myself clearly. My child wasn't dying of cancer or wearing cables because of leukemia. They were going to enable Amber to walk correctly one day, and what I needed to do was seek God's forgiveness and be grateful for those cables. *Oh, God,* I prayed, *please forgive me for my foolishness, pride, and impatience. Thank you for the precious gift of Amber Joy exactly as she is. Thank you for those twister cables and for the promise that they represent. I am so grateful, Lord.*

Every six weeks we went to see the orthopedist, and at each visit I would anxiously wait for a positive progress report. But he always said the same thing: "We may be able to have her out of them in time for kindergarten."

Summertime came and I was determined to have Amber potty-trained before she turned two in August. However, it was impossible with only a two-hour break without the cables each day. By the time Amber indicated that she needed to "go" and we rushed to the bathroom and got everything unbuckled, those shoes would be wet again. It seemed hopeless. With her birthday fast approaching, I decided that if it was going to take four years to straighten those legs, then we deserved a *four-* hour break per day from the cables: two in the morning and two in the afternoon to help us triumph with potty training. I felt guilty, knowing that we had an appointment with the orthopedist at the end of the August. Surely he would notice her lack of progress with the brace, but at the rate we were going, her shoes would be ruined before she outgrew them.

That summer wasn't just challenging at home, it was challenging economically. My husband's young law practice was very busy, but many clients neglected to pay their bills on time so money was tight. Without my working with him full-time, we had hired extra help, and the financial challenges made us very conscious of our dependence on the Lord.

• • •

The afternoon of Amber's August doctor appointment was hot and humid, and we didn't have air-conditioning. She was down for a nap, and I was stressed. We had been victorious with the potty training, but I dreaded facing the doctor and confessing that I had allowed her extra hours out of the cables. Our appointment wasn't until three PM, and I was grateful that Amber would be rested and less likely to be fussy during the appointment. Putting the matter temporarily out of my mind, I reached for my Bible.

I had been studying the book of Exodus and the character of Moses. A longing swept over me, and I slipped to my knees and cried out to God that hot afternoon, praying, "O, Lord, so often you showed your power to Moses in unmistakable ways. I long to see your power at work in an unmistakable way in *my* life too!"

Having said those words, I sat back on the floor and looked around my living room feeling a little sheepish. I thought to myself, *And just what do you think you were asking God for, Jennie? Do you think you're going to win the Publishers Clearing House sweepstakes?*

Noting the time, I hurried to wake Amber and pushed her in her stroller to the hospital for her appointment with the orthopedist. In the examining room, I went through the ritual of unstrapping her cables and undressing her down to a shirt and the training panties that we had been so proud of before this appointment.

Greeting us when he came in, the doctor lifted Amber to the end of the examining table. Holding each calf, he applied pressure, twisting slightly while Amber fussed and reached for me. She hated that part of the exam. I opened my mouth to confess that I had given her the extra two-hour break with the cables for potty training, but I didn't even get a chance. "Interesting . . . ," he said. "Mrs. Dimkoff, I'd like to see her walk a distance down the hospital corridor. Why don't you stand several doors down and urge her to come to you, and I'll observe from here?"

And so, without the cables, Amber happily toddled down the hallway to me and away from the doctor! "Very good!" The doctor said. "Now, I want to watch her do that again. Let's switch places." Once again, Amber hurried down the corridor without falling. Back in the examining room, the doctor examined her X-rays and legs once more and said, "This is truly remarkable. Would you like to buy Amber some new shoes?"

I was confused. "You mean we need to order a new pair of orthopedic shoes?" She was close to outgrowing the old ones, and they looked disgusting.

The doctor smiled. "No. Actually, your daughter's progress is nothing short of remarkable! She doesn't *need* the braces anymore. How would you like to buy her a pair of sneakers to finish out the summer?"

I was so stunned I could barely speak—not just because of what he had told me but because I was remembering that just an hour before, I had been on my knees in my living room asking God to allow me to see his power at work in an unmistakable way.

I can't remember what I said, but I do remember putting Amber into the stroller and pushing her all the way down-town to Vredeveld's Shoe Store to check out the sneaker selec-tion. Then, with Amber wearing her bright new shoes and the braces hanging off the back of the stroller, I jubilantly pushed Amber the rest of the way downtown to her father's law office so we could surprise Graydon.

As the months went by, we delighted in asking Amber Joy two questions:

"Hey, little girl, where did you get those big brown eyes?"

Her response was always, "I got these from my daddy!"

"And where did you get those beautiful straight legs?"

With a grin that lit up her face she'd respond, "I got these legs from Jesus!"

No correction was ever required.

Many years have passed since that memorable day, but a child-sized brace still hangs from a hook in our garage with small scuffed shoes dangling from cables as a reminder of God's gift.

Call to me and I will answer you, and show you great and mighty things you do not know.

—JEREMIAH 33:3 KJV

> Never be afraid to trust an unknown
> future to a known God.[1]
> —CORRIE TEN BOOM

CHAPTER 27

Sunday Morning Surprise

BY CAROL KENT

Debbie's heart was heavy. She had tried to make a difficult marriage work, but she could no longer make excuses for her abusive husband. Her decision to seek a divorce was one of the most difficult of her life. Four months later she packed up her car and moved across the country with her children, ages five and eight. They took very little with them—two suitcases filled with clothing and another filled with the children's favorite toys. Debbie knew they needed to start over in a safe place in a different city.

Finding a good job was a high priority now that Debbie was the only breadwinner. It didn't take her long to get hired by the Interpreting Service for the Deaf. She was thrilled with this opportunity. Debbie knew sign language well, and she loved talking with deaf people. This was her chance to work with them on a daily basis and to provide much-needed assistance at the same time. It was an answer to her prayers to find work that matched her skills perfectly and would also provide the necessary finances for her family's needs.

Just a few weeks into her new job, she noticed that her car was making some unusual noises on her drive home. That evening it chugged to a halt, and no matter how many times she tried to start the engine, it wouldn't turn over. Debbie was hardworking, intelligent, and creative, but she knew nothing about the mechanics of automobiles. Later, she discovered that her vehicle had been leaking oil, and the repairs would cost more than the car was worth. She urgently needed reliable transportation to get to her new job, but she was struggling to make ends meet. That day, her frustration became a prayer: "Lord, I don't know where to turn. My kids and I have been through so much pain. You've provided a place for us to live and you've already opened the door for a fulfilling job for me, but I desperately need a reliable car to get to work, and I have no money. Please give me wisdom. I don't know anyone who can help me."

While hurriedly finishing her prayer, Debbie wiped a stray tear. Then she suddenly remembered seeing a FOR SALE sign in the window of a car in the church parking lot on the previous Sunday. Her mind began spinning with ideas: *Maybe I could clean for the owner of the car and work to pay off the purchase price over time. I know I can't afford to buy a car right now, but maybe whoever put that car up for sale will be willing to work with me on a flexible payment plan.*

Debbie called the pastor of the church and told him about her need for a vehicle. She asked if he knew who owned the car that had the FOR SALE sign in the window. Debbie was sorry to hear that he had no idea who the owner was, but he quickly encouraged her by saying, "Please plan on coming to church next week. I'll arrange for someone to pick you and the children up."

When Sunday arrived, they were ready to go, and the promised transportation was provided. They had not been going to this church very long, but Debbie had already joined the choir. After their song that morning, the pastor stood up to pray. He mentioned a few specific needs in the congregation, and then, quite unexpectedly, he called Debbie's name and asked her to step down from the choir loft and join him in front of the platform so the church could pray for her need of a car.

A momentary wave of embarrassment swept over Debbie as she walked down the steps from the choir loft to the designated place at the front of the sanctuary. Then a sweet peace swept over her, and she felt at ease as she stood in front of the pastor.

He said, "I'd like to ask a few of our deacons and others who would like to join us to come and pray for Debbie right now." In a tasteful and appropriate way he told the people in the congregation about some of the struggles she'd come through and that she had recently found a better job, but she urgently needed a car. Then he prayed, asking God to meet her need as quickly as possible.

As the pastor finished praying for her, a white-haired man standing in the back row of the choir stepped down and walked over to the pastor. Before saying a word, he placed a set of keys on the podium and said, "Pastor, while you were praying God spoke to me and asked me to give Debbie my car. My wife and I drove to church separately today because I needed to be here early. So she can take it home with her. All I ask is that she let me get my golf clubs out of the trunk."

A low chuckle could be heard from the congregation, along with a few *amens* and *hallelujahs*.

Tears clouded Debbie's eyes as she experienced God's amazing provision. Later, she said, "I didn't even know this man's name, even though we both sang in the church choir, but God touched his heart with my need and he stepped forward to offer what he had. In addition to giving me this generous gift, he allowed me to keep the license plates on the car and continued paying for the insurance coverage until I could afford to pay it myself."

In the middle of moving into a new community, getting her children established in a different school system, struggling to pay her bills, and starting a new job, Debbie experienced a powerful truth. God knew her needs, heard her cry for help, touched the heart of a stranger, and provided her with exactly what she needed.

And this same God who takes care of me will supply all your needs from his glorious riches, which have been given to us in Christ Jesus.

—PHILIPPIANS 4:19 NLT

Let the past sleep, but let it sleep on
the bosom of Christ, and go out into
the irresistible future with Him.[1]
—OSWALD CHAMBERS

CHAPTER 28

The Ring

BY JENNIE AFMAN DIMKOFF

Tanya stepped uncertainly into the monthly ladies' ministry meeting at the church she and her husband, Luke, had been attending for a short time. Normally, she considered herself a people person, but after being deeply hurt in a previous church she was not eager to make herself vulnerable in this new setting and held her heart very much in reserve. She slipped into a seat near the back, kept quiet, and just tried to blend in.

A woman from the congregation shared a meaningful message that day, and Tanya was thankful for the encouragement. She enjoyed hearing the woman's testimony and planned to apply what she had learned to her own life. At the end of her message, however, Tanya was taken off guard. The woman held up a ring.

It was a beautiful ring with a simple gold band and three diamond-shaped amethysts mounted side by side. She told the audience that as she prayed while preparing her message that morning, the Lord had impressed upon her to bring the ring, because it was his desire to give it to one of the women who would be attending the meeting. At the conclusion of her message she smiled and announced, "Tanya, the Lord wants me to give this ring to *you*."

Tanya was stunned and then filled with an emotion that almost overwhelmed her. Right there in the middle of a group of women, many of whom she didn't even know, God had chosen to share a very special, amazingly memorable father-daughter moment with her.

"Thank you," Tanya managed to whisper. And with a trembling hand she reached out and accepted the ring. *Will it fit me?* she wondered. Her heart was thundering as she slipped it on her finger, and a moment later she burst into tears.

It was as if the ring had been made for her. It fit perfectly. The other women in the room couldn't possibly know the significance of that moment in Tanya's life, but she would never forget it as long as she lived. Her heavenly father had presented her with her very own purity ring.

As Tanya had grown from a small child into a young teen she had endured the neglect of her drug-addicted mother and horrible abuse at the hands of the adult men her mother invited into their lives. The thought of a loving father was beyond what she could fathom. Instead, there had only been glimpses of longing and moments of contemplation, in which she had allowed herself to imagine what it might be like to experience an appropriate father-daughter relationship. One of those longings had been to have a father who truly loved her and treated her like a princess. While in high school she knew Christian girls whose fathers had given them beautiful rings called purity rings. Later, when they married, those rings were exchanged for wedding rings from their husbands. She secretly longed for a father who would give her a beautiful ring that would represent that father-daughter love relationship. The ring, she imagined, would make her feel special, loved, and pure. Needless to say, with the abuse in her background, it was a pipe dream that Tanya had simply tucked away in her heart. She had never shared those feelings with others. Only the Lord knew the longing of her heart.

Tanya had come to know the Lord as a teenager and was nineteen when she met and married twenty-one-year-old Luke.

She loved him dearly, and Luke was a godly young man whose unconditional love for her and strength as he patiently walked with her through flashbacks and breakdowns only made her love him more. For years she struggled to trust the worthy man God had brought into her life because of her history. Luke loved her in spite of all that, and he was patient when she struggled with feelings of her own worthlessness.

However, that morning, when the woman who led the Bible study presented Tanya with the beautiful ring as a gift from God, Tanya couldn't have imagined feeling any more special or loved. She began to weep, knowing at that moment that the Lord had seen her—fulfilling a desire of her heart in a way that she never could have expected. Real healing began taking place in her life. Years of longing began fading away, and in its place healing found a home in her heart.

Tanya loved the ring, but it was so much more to her than a lovely piece of jewelry. The abuse and shame of her past had blinded her to the fact that because of Jesus, she was indeed pure in God's sight.

She studied the ring that was now sparkling on her finger, hardly able to believe it was really hers. Then a thought came to her that she accepted as her own special message. "The purple stones are the color of *royalty*," she whispered with joy-filled wonder. Tanya laughed out loud as the tears kept falling. She was a princess too! She was the daughter of the King of Kings!

Every good gift and every perfect gift is from above, and comes down from the Father.

—JAMES 1:17A KJV

What does love look like? It has the hands to help others. It has the feet to hasten to the poor and needy. It has eyes to see misery and want. It has the ears to hear the sighs and sorrows of men. That is what love looks like.[1]

—AUGUSTINE

CHAPTER 29

Showered with Love

BY CAROL KENT

Stephen and Loidys were eighteen years old and expecting a baby when they were married in a simple ceremony. Loidys's relatives were surprised by the news of the baby, but they were happy for her. Stephen's family, however, was not so thrilled. All but one of them arrived at the wedding wearing black. Later, when she reviewed the photographs, Loidys thought, *If I wasn't in a wedding dress, you'd think the people in this picture were attending a funeral.*

By the time Loidys was five months into her pregnancy, she and Stephen decided to move to an area where there were better job opportunities. They drove a U-Haul truck from Miami, Florida, to New York City in mid-February. The farther north they traveled, the more they realized they were not properly prepared for freezing temperatures. Since they were from South Florida, thoughts of cold weather had not occurred to them.

It was snowing when they finally arrived in the state of New York at midnight. All they had left was $100, so stopping at a motel was totally out of the question. Their plan was to get to a home owned by Stephen's mother in Ronkonkoma, Long Island. They were exhausted but kept on driving until they reached their destination. Upon arrival, they found themselves in a freezing-cold house. There was a fireplace, so Stephen found some old furniture in the attic and broke it apart to make a fire. After unloading a mattress from the truck, they fell asleep in front of the fireplace until the frigid temperatures woke them up a few hours later.

The promised job opportunity didn't work out, and within a month they had to move out of the house. On borrowed money they rented a guesthouse on the island, but two months later they were evicted because they couldn't afford the rent.

Stephen's grandmother lived in Queens, and he asked her if they, or even just Loidys, could stay with her until they could find a place to live. Grandma declined, saying, "I just got new sofas, and I really don't want anyone to sleep on them." A week later some relatives arrived from Colombia—and *they* were invited to sleep on Grandma's lovely sofas.

Loidys knew that in the eyes of Stephen's family, she had ruined his promising future. One of Stephen's aunts was over-heard saying, "That girl probably got pregnant on purpose!" It was clear to Loidys that she was not wanted. Her sense of rejection was wide and deep and penetratingly hurtful.

Then another relative, Stephen's great-aunt Luz, took pity on them and invited them to stay in her home, where she also housed a multitude of other relatives. Soon after, Stephen got a job in the shipping department of a textile warehouse in Man-hattan. He earned $168 a week, which enabled them to help Aunt Luz out with groceries. Loidys was now eight months pregnant and felt unsafe and unloved. People surrounded her, but she was lonely. It was especially difficult during the week-days when her husband was at work.

Loidys went into labor shortly after midnight on July 8. She and Stephen had gone to a movie, and after they returned to the house, her water broke. The labor was short, and she delivered a beautiful baby girl at six AM. Her joyful thoughts tumbled out with great emotion: *My baby is perfect and gorgeous. She looks like an angel.* They named her Stephanie. A couple of

Steve's relatives came to the hospital to visit, but most showed no interest in welcoming the new baby into their family.

Steve was allowed one unpaid day to be at the hospital with his wife and baby, but he had to go back to work the next morning. On the day Loidys was to be released from the hospital, she didn't have anyone to pick her up. Quite unexpectedly, Amanda, a woman Loidys had met earlier, volunteered to provide transportation. Loidys gratefully accepted her offer.

She knew Amanda was a very nice, religious lady who often went to church and prayed a lot. She had a caring disposition and was friendly. Loidys didn't know Amanda well, but she remembered one occasion when she had visited Amanda. Loidys had sat in her kitchen and watched Amanda cook while they talked. There was something kind and comforting about the way this compassionate woman had reached out to her.

Amanda picked Loidys and baby Stephanie up at the hospital and drove back to her own home. As Loidys walked into the house, she saw lots of people she didn't know, and in unison they yelled, "Surprise!" Unbeknownst to Loidys, Amanda had planned a baby shower in her honor. Loidys couldn't believe her eyes. With joy she realized what was happening: *These strangers have gathered to give* me *presents! They came to celebrate the birth of my baby girl!*

Loidys was speechless and overwhelmed with gratitude. These wonderful people not only showered her with gifts, but they also showered her with love. They provided her with everything she and Stephen needed to care for their newborn daughter. That day Loidys was blessed with the kindness of a caring person who saw her need, engaged friends in an act of selfless love, and splashed acceptance, joy, and celebration on her life.

• • •

Fifteen years later, following multiple moves, the family went back to New York. The baby, now grown, had asked for a trip to the city of her birth for her fifteenth birthday celebration. Stephen and Loidys took Stephanie to the hospital where she was born and to the places where they had lived. Loidys made an emotional call to Amanda and thanked her for the lavish love and kindness she had showered on a first-time mother who was in great need emotionally, spiritually, and financially.

Loidys says, "I felt so lonely and rejected. God showed up and touched my baby girl and me that day through the kindness of Amanda. I know he was there and I was not alone. He loved me and provided for me through the hearts and hands of people who loved him."

I have loved you with an everlasting love; I have drawn you with loving-kindness.

—JEREMIAH 31:3B NIV

People often consider thoughts to be fleeting and worthless, but yours are so precious to Me that I remain ever near you, reading each one.[1]

—SARAH YOUNG

CHAPTER 30

Shopping with God

BY JENNIE AFMAN DIMKOFF

It was a beautiful California afternoon, and Michelle Peel, the director of alumni relations at Multnomah University, needed to go shopping. She planned to attend a wedding later that week and needed to find a new dress to wear to the event. Thinking it would definitely be more fun to shop with a friend, she decided to ask her triplet sister, Danielle, to join her.

"Hey, Nel! Want to hit the mall with me this afternoon?"

Because of other responsibilities, Danielle was not able to join Michelle.

"Buy something for me, though!" she said with a grin in her voice.

"I'll see what I can do," Michelle murmured back, and sighed. Christmas wasn't too far away and she knew that Nel had been eyeing Liz Claiborne purses for some time. She made a mental note to look for a purse for Nel while she was out.

Michelle was single and normally very independent. It shouldn't have been any problem shopping alone, but that day felt different. She really longed for a shopping buddy. As she got into the car and headed out, she decided to invite the Lord to join her on her shopping adventure. Michelle realized the unusual nature of such an invitation. God might have far more important things on his schedule for that day, but, after thinking about it, she decided *that* was what she loved about him the most. No matter how many things were on his to-do list, God always made time for her. It felt as if there was not another thing that he would rather be doing than spending the afternoon with her.

As she drove along, Michelle carried on a conversation with God. *Lord, I need to find a dress for my friend's wedding. Can you please help me today? I don't feel great about it, because I never seem to have success when I shop under the pressure of time constraints. I hate to bother you with such a little thing when you have major global concerns, but I know you care about the little things too.*

Michelle felt like God responded to her, asking her exactly what she was looking for. His voice wasn't audible; it was a still, small voice in the back of her head that she heard often when they were in quiet conversation. She began to describe the dress that she had in mind, one in a trendy style with a fresh, updated look.

Well, I'm thinking that a capped sleeve off the shoulder with a small strap that comes across the top of the shoulder would be lovely. Oh, and a fitted bodice and a flowing A-line skirt would be perfect, Lord. What color? Wow, Lord! You're not only interested in the style I'd like but the color as well?

Michelle suddenly knew that this was one of those faith-teaching moments, where the Lord was teaching her to trust him in the smallest of things. So, taking a breath, she swallowed and told him, *A floral pastel was the picture that I had in mind. And, God, you know that I am on a tight budget right now. I can't afford an expensive dress.*

Again that quiet voice came: "How much would you like to spend?"

Forty dollars, Michelle responded. She knew it would be difficult to find a decent gown for that small amount, but nonetheless that is what she could afford and he *had* asked.

Michelle had been headed to a popular mall, but as she drove along, she felt a strong urging from the Lord to take the next freeway exit. It was several exits before the mall where she had originally been headed and she wasn't sure why she was taking the exit, but she obeyed. She noticed a strip mall to her right that she wasn't familiar with and felt the Lord encouraging her to stop at the first store. Her interest perked up considerably when she pulled into the parking lot and could see a large printed sign in the store window: LIZ CLAIBORNE PURSES 40–60% OFF ORIGINAL PRICES!

"Wow!" she whispered. "God, you are amazing! This must be the reason you wanted me to stop here!" As she entered the department store, red sale signs led her in the direction of the handbags. As she approached, there it was: the *exact* purse that Nel had been eyeing at the mall—and in the perfect navy blue hue. Best of all, it was 60 percent off!

As she excitedly headed to the checkout with the purse in hand, Michelle felt the Lord telling her to look in the clothing section. This was not a department store that she frequented, so she didn't realize they carried clothing as well. As she approached the first rack, she was shocked to find the exact dress she had described to the Lord in the car just moments before. Could it be he had directed her there to find her dress as well? With great excitement and without even looking at the tag, she put the dress over her arm and raced to the dressing room. It fit perfectly! As another customer in the dressing area zipped her up, Michelle felt so amazed by what had happened that she said enthusiastically, "This is a 'God moment'! It is *exactly* what I told God I was looking for!" She may have alarmed the other customer a bit with all of her enthusiasm, but Michelle couldn't help it. God had answered her prayer and she just had to share the experience.

With her treasures in hand, Michelle headed for the checkout. She had been so excited about finding the Liz Claiborne purse and then also the perfect dress in the exact color and size that she hadn't even thought to look at the price tag. Looking down at the tag, a huge grin spread across her face. God hadn't missed a beat. The price on the dress was $39.99.

Michelle had taken great joy in inviting God to spend time shopping with her that afternoon. He, in turn, had blessed her by providing even more than what she had asked for that day!

Delight yourself in the Lord and He will give you the desires of your heart.

—PSALM 37:4 NIV

Faith is not a storm cellar to which men and women can flee for refuge from the storms of life. It is, instead, an inner force that gives them the strength to face those storms and their consequences with serenity of spirit.[1]

—SAM J. ERVIN JR.

CHAPTER 31

The Intimidating Traveler

BY CAROL KENT

Cynthia struggled with fear. She didn't like to come home to a dark house alone at night, and strange noises in the middle of the night terrorized her. But her biggest fear, the one that paralyzed her, was her fear of crashing while flying in an airplane.

This, coupled with her creative imagination, wreaked havoc on Cynthia's mind—especially when flying was unavoidable. She often turned down expense-paid trips that required reaching her destination by air. As her children grew older and moved far from home, it eventually became unavoidable for her to get on a plane.

Shortly after September 11, 2001, Cynthia was facing another dreaded flight—but she was willing to face her fears in order to spend time with her son on the West Coast. Glancing to her left at the far end of the ticket counter she saw a turbaned young man, away from the lines of travelers eager to unload their baggage and obtain boarding passes. As Cynthia gazed in his direction, she became aware of the backpack he carried. He nervously and repeatedly glanced at his watch. Cynthia's deep-seated anxiety that had begun to churn three weeks prior to the trip now raced into red-alert level. Silently and desperately she prayed, *Lord, please make certain this young man is not on my plane.*

Cynthia's daughter suggested she take some pills that would help her relax. She disliked taking medication but followed her daughter's advice. She quickly swallowed a pill, hoping it would calm her anxious heart, but she could feel herself slipping into full-blown panic.

With check-in now completed and her boarding pass tucked safely in her carry-on luggage, she held tightly to her husband. They kissed and had a lingering, tearful good-bye. While waiting to pass through security, she removed her jacket and shoes and placed her bag on the screening belt. Looking ahead, she immediately caught sight of the man in the turban. He was at the end of the line directly ahead of her.

Cynthia prayed. *Lord, please make this man's backpack activate the alarm. Help someone to see what a threat he is to the security of this airport.* Cynthia began unpacking her own bulging, brown leather bag for inspection, while keeping a close eye on the man ahead of her in the line. Suddenly the alarms went off and Cynthia was sure they'd caught the man with contraband. But to her dismay, he got all the way through security, and she discovered it was her own metal objects that had triggered the alarm.

She waited in a holding area while the security personnel searched her bag. After being cleared, Cynthia put her shoes back on and repacked her bag. Finally, she was on her way down the concourse with a full hour before her departure time.

Once Cynthia arrived at the gate, to her horror, she saw the man in the turban waiting for the same plane. Nervously, she watched him as he sat alone staring out the window, periodically checking his watch, as he had earlier. He got up, and Cynthia positioned herself so she could see where he was going and who he was meeting. The man disappeared briefly into the restroom and returned to his seat. Cynthia prayed for someone to come and pull this young man from the crowd of travelers.

When it was time to board, Cynthia decided she would be one of the last passengers to get on the plane. Her eyes were fixed on the man in the turban and she watched as he handed his ticket to the smiling airline attendant and stepped on the plane. *Oh, God, please no, no; this cannot be what you have prepared for me,* she thought. Fear shot through Cynthia's entire being, crippling her ability to think rationally.

The final boarding call bellowed through the loudspeakers, and Cynthia made herself move toward the plane, knowing her son would be waiting for her at the end of this dreaded flight. The "miracle pill" she took earlier had not reduced her anxiety. At the doorway into the plane, she handed her boarding pass to the flight attendant, and through tears she asked for help in locating her seat. Arriving at the right row, she was stunned to see that the man in the turban was already in the window seat—right next to her seat!

Thinking quickly, Cynthia decided to place her bag on the floor, instead of in the overhead compartment. *I might need to use it to block him if he becomes threatening and tries to leave his seat,* she thought.

As Cynthia sat in quiet, tearful submission to her present situation, she realized that God had allowed this seating arrangement for a purpose. She found herself praying the very same prayer Mary prayed when the angel Gabriel gave her a shocking announcement: "Be it unto me according to your word."[2] Silently Cynthia continued. *Lord, use me in any way you can. I am available to be your heart, your hands, your ears, and your mouth during this flight.*

When it became obvious to Cynthia that her unexpected seatmate had to do with a plan bigger than she anticipated, she began to pray again. *Lord, I am giving you my fear. I acknowledge your sovereignty over every detail of life. Here am I; use me.* She felt an unforeseen calm. Her traveling companion sat staring out the window as he occasionally looked at his watch. Again, Cynthia wondered why he had such an obsession with time. Momentarily she gave in to fear again. *Does something have to happen at just the precise moment so his terror plot takes place on schedule?*

Suddenly Cynthia found herself leaning in the direction of the stranger and asking, "Would you like to be quiet on this trip or would you like to talk?"

Now, Lord, the ball is in your court, she thought.

The young man's prompt reply surprised her. Looking up, he said, "I would like to talk." With the door to conversation wide open, Cynthia began with simple questions:

> *"Tell me about yourself. Where are you from?"*
> *"Do you have family in the Spokane area?"*
> *"What is the significance of your turban?"*

The man respectfully responded to her queries as he told her the entire story of his journey from India to the United States. She learned he was in his midtwenties and had grown up as a Sikh in a religious home that advocated the pursuit of salvation through disciplined, personal meditation on the name and message of God. He had come to America searching for a good job. None of his family members were in the USA, and he was completely alone in a foreign land filled with people who had repeatedly handed him alienation and rejection. He had made the United States his home in a post–September 11 haze of anxiety and fear. Sadly, Cynthia knew she had been one of those people who had misjudged him.

He asked Cynthia about her life and faith, and a three-hour plane trip became an exchange of two contrasting worldviews. They both described lifestyles that were very different. Cynthia's heart warmed to this young man. He was close to the age of her son, and she realized she could offer him the gift of friendship.

The flight was over too quickly, and as they exited the plane, Cynthia gave him a book that further explained biblical Christianity. The young man was an eager learner, and his home was near the home of Cynthia's son. She invited him to their Thanksgiving dinner. He was too shy to attend the reunion, but he visited them a day later.

Cynthia learned something new about herself and something remarkable about God that day. She had allowed fear to cloud her vision and prejudice her opinions, but through this experience, Cynthia was finally free to embrace the serenity that only comes when we rest in God, knowing he has a plan far beyond what we can see. Throughout the past eight years, this friendship that started on a three-hour plane trip has continued to develop, with an ongoing exchange about the young Indian's religious commitments and the Christian faith of Cynthia and her family.

Do not fear, for I am with you; do not anxiously
look about you, for I am your God. I will
strengthen you; surely I will help you. Surely I will
uphold you with My righteous right hand.

—ISAIAH 41:10 NASB

> When we bring sunshine into the lives of
> others we're warmed by it ourselves. When we
> spill a little happiness, it splashes on us.[1]
> —BARBARA JOHNSON

CHAPTER 32

The Favorite

BY JENNIE AFMAN DIMKOFF

It was two days before Christmas, but even with the busyness of the holidays and over an hour to travel, I wouldn't have missed the funeral of my favorite aunt for the world. Aunt Deal was ninety-two years old when she passed away. The last elderly person's funeral I had attended was very small because most of the deceased's friends and immediate family had already passed on, but that was not the case with this funeral. The place was *packed,* and people crowded in, standing in the back and along one wall. Holiday or no holiday, people wanted to pay their respects to Aunt Deal.

My mother had ten siblings, so I had a lot of aunts. All of them were wonderful, but it was Aunt Deal who *never* forgot my birthday. (Actually she was the only aunt who remembered it at all.) Back when the Tooth Fairy was paying a nickel per tooth, Aunt Deal would enclose a whole quarter in my birthday card. I'd get that card in the mail, and sometimes I'd just hold it without breaking the seal, feeling that quarter through the envelope and loving her for remembering. She would sign it "Happy Birthday, Jennie Beth! Love, Aunt Deal X O X O," and I could feel her hugs and kisses across the miles. When I was ten, she started sending *two* quarters, and those envelopes kept coming until I graduated from high school and left for college. (When she turned eighty, I wrote her a letter and told her how much those cards and quarters had meant to me, and I filled her card with postage stamps and beautiful stickers. I just wanted to send *her* a big fat kiss in a card for a change!)

Aunt Deal and Uncle Jake had two sons and two daughters. Dolly and Jean were my gorgeous, older "girl" cousins, and I remember thinking that they were about the most glamorous girls I had ever seen! But, even better than that, they were *nice*. They were so kind and loving whenever we would come to visit. They were just as gracious and lovely as their mom, and they never seemed to mind that I was her favorite niece and got special attention. However, as I grew older, I realized that all of my sisters and several of my other cousins thought that *they* were Aunt Deal's favorite nieces! At first I was a bit jealous, but over time, I realized that Aunt Deal had enough love to share with all of us.

When I stepped into the funeral home on that cold December afternoon, the first thing I noticed was that all of Aunt Deal's daughters and daughters-in-law, and many of her grandchildren, had worn red because that was her favorite color. They weren't there to grieve her passing. They were there to celebrate her life and her home-going to heaven! The pastor's message was fine, but what really made the service wonderful was when her children and grandchildren got up, one after another, and shared lessons they had learned from her or precious memories they had about her. Some were:

- *That people are more important than things or schedules.*
- *That to know and love God is the most important decision you can make in life.*
- *That there is always time to stop for a good cup of coffee (and that windmill cookies are the cookie of choice to go with it).*
- *That the seat next to Aunt Deal was the coveted spot at*

*church. (One reason was that there was an endless supply
of candy in her purse that made it easier to sit through the
pastor's lengthy sermons.)*

- *That "pumps" made a young girl's legs look feminine,
and that Aunt Deal's closet was full of high heels to wear
while parading around her house. (Plus, the closet at
the end of the hall had a mink coat and stole that were
available to add to "the look" for dress-up tea parties at
her house.)*

- *That the family would give her red geraniums for
Christmas because those were her favorites, and somehow
when summer rolled around, she'd have babied those
geraniums through the winter and have them looking
perfect for summer planting.*

After her children and grandchildren spoke, others got
up with their tributes to Aunt Deal, and—weepy me—I cried
through them all but loved every minute. I was tempted to get
up and tell everyone about how much those birthday cards
had meant to me growing up, but there were so many other
people with memories to share that I just listened. It occurred
to me as I sat there that I wasn't the only person in the room
who had tagged Aunt Deal as their favorite aunt or grandma,
neighbor or friend. Aunt Deal had been somebody special to
a lot of people.

What had made her such a remarkable woman? Widowed
at age fifty-two, Aunt Deal could have been bitter, frustrated
with life, or too busy with just "getting by" to take time for me
or anyone else for that matter, but that wasn't the case at all.
She loved and served God, and she made time for her children
and grandchildren and so many others. She went to work at
the Radio Bible Class in Grand Rapids, Michigan, and worked
for that international ministry until she retired at age seventy.

Until the day she died, she had a twinkle in her eye and love in her heart for others.

My last memory of Aunt Deal is at a large family reunion. I was probably the chubbiest I had ever been, and I debated for some time over what to wear. Trying to choose something that would be slenderizing, I finally decided on cropped pants and a fitted jacket. When we arrived, Aunt Deal held out her arms, and kissing me on the cheek, she said, "Oh, Jennie, aren't you just the cutest thing I've seen all day! I'm so glad you're here, honey."

She was in her nineties and I was in my fifties, and overweight or not, because I was held in Aunt Deal's loving embrace, I felt gorgeous! She still had the gift of making me feel special. God used Aunt Deal throughout my lifetime to bless me with a note in a card or an encouraging word. She surprised me by showing up at speaking engagements and sat down with me at reunions and held my hand and inquired about my current projects. In so many other ways, time and again, she was God's affirming touch in my life. I wonder if she realized the role model she was to me.

I determined years ago that *I* would become the favorite aunt to my nieces and nephews. I knew I would have some tough competition because my sisters are pretty wonderful, but I wanted to be like Aunt Deal and bless the lives of my nieces and nephews like she had mine. I found out that it takes an investment of time, but the rewards are great. If my grown nephews needed a meal or a place to bunk on the weekend, they knew they were welcome, and every Monday when my sister Joy brought her youngest three children into town for piano lessons (their piano teacher lived next door to my house) they would stay with me until it was time for them to head next door. What fun we had!

Over the years, I've learned that giving gifts wasn't the key to being the favorite aunt to my nieces and nephews. Instead, I needed to:

- *Love them unconditionally.*
- *Pray for them faithfully.*
- *Listen to what they had to say.*
- *Send them an occasional card with a personal note. (Snail mail through the postal service is almost a gift these days.)*
- *Stop what I am doing and play with them when we were together.*
- *Remember their birthdays.*
- *Open my home for meals and conversation as they grew older.*

The truth is all of my sisters are so wonderful that I've decided it might be too painful for them if our nieces and nephews actually give *me* the title of most favored aunt. (Shucks!) I'm just hoping the majority of them will read this story and keep the secret to themselves until they give it away by wearing red to my funeral!

Jesus said, "Let the little children come to me, and do not hinder them, for the kingdom of heaven belongs to such as these."

—MATTHEW 19:14 NIV

> When God is involved, anything can
> happen. Be open. Stay that way.[1]
> —CHARLES SWINDOLL

CHAPTER 33

The Long Drive Home

BY CAROL KENT

Stephanie had begun a new job that necessitated a long commute. On weekdays she lived in a rented studio apartment in Atlanta, but each weekend she made the tedious, five-hour trip back to her home in Jacksonville. She knew the route well.

One Friday afternoon as she was headed back to Florida, Stephanie thought about the most recent lesson from her women's Bible study. The theme was choosing contentment, expecting God to surprise you, and being open to his leading. But that day Stephanie was stuck in a pit of discouragement that bordered on flat-out depression.

She was lonely after leaving an exciting job that required her to be with customers and coworkers at social gatherings. The new job made her feel isolated. At the time Stephanie made the decision to leave her former employment, she believed God was leading her to quit, but now regret and despair had replaced her earlier confidence. She particularly missed attending the national sales meetings—and this Friday her trip was even more difficult because her former colleagues were gathering for one of their major events.

Driving along the highway, she cried out to God: *Why am I here? I don't like being all by myself week after week! Why did you lead me to leave that last job and take this position? I wish I knew I made the right decision.*

At that moment she noticed the lyrics of the Third Day CD she was listening to in the car. They were singing about a light at the end of the tunnel and belted out, "There's so much you're living for!"

Yeah, right, Stephanie thought, *I don't seem to be living for very much right now.* She knew it was going to be a long drive home, and she needed to think about something else. Tears began filling her eyes and spilling onto her cheeks. Glancing out the window, she noticed a large dog along the highway. He appeared to be a hefty pit bull–Rottweiler mix. Then she saw a hitchhiker nearby in army fatigues.

A mile later Stephanie heard an all-too-familiar *thump, thump, thump.* The sound matched her mood as she rolled her eyes and thought, *Not again! This is my third flat tire this year! Give me a break!* She pulled her SUV off to the side of the road and began the well-practiced drill of pulling out her spare tire, jacking up the car, and preparing to change the tire. Before long the hitchhiker and his dog came up to the side of her car, and the young man offered to help. Together they got the job done quickly.

Stephanie asked him to share his story. He said he couldn't get a ride on the big rigs because of the new security laws and his dog wasn't allowed on buses. She learned he had been traveling from Nashville when his car broke down, and he was headed to Miami, where he had been promised a job.

Fear cast a shadow over Stephanie as she pondered what to do. It was still light outside, but she knew it was dangerous to pick up hitchhikers. The man *had* helped her change the tire, but she knew almost nothing about his background—and he had a sizable, potentially aggressive dog.

With much hesitation and a prayer, she offered to drive the man and his dog down the road a few miles. Dozer, the hairy half of this unlikely hitchhiking duo, jumped into the backseat while the young man settled into the front passenger seat. Moments later Dozer began to give Stephanie continuous wet, sloppy dog kisses on her cheek and all over the right side of her head. She couldn't help but chuckle as the dog lavished affection on her. Stephanie's depressed mood started lifting.

Still, it made her nervous and insecure to think that she had picked up a total stranger. As she turned the engine on, the CD that had played earlier began where it left off. Suddenly the young man in army fatigues spoke up: "I love Third Day! Their music really encourages me—and you've encouraged me too. You are the first person who has picked us up in days. Dozer and I have been sleeping under bridges and in the woods. You are really a blessing!"

Stephanie listened attentively to him as they passed several police cars along the highway. She believed she had done the right thing and thought she would take him as far as the next exit. Then, simultaneously, they both saw a billboard. In large letters it said: THIS IS A SIGN FROM GOD.

He said, "See, you were supposed to get that flat tire, and you were supposed to pick me up!" They laughed and continued their conversation for the next couple of hours, stopping only once for something to eat. The man talked about his family and how he was injured in the war. Stephanie learned that when he returned home from the war in Iraq with injuries, his wife left him, taking their two children and the better of their two cars, leaving him with the car that broke down earlier on his journey.

Stephanie wasn't sure where she would drop him off. The afternoon sun was disappearing and she knew it would be dark soon. As they approached the Florida state line, she silently prayed: *God, please let there be a hotel at the next exit that accepts dogs. Give me wisdom about what to do.* She pulled off the highway at the last exit before she had to head east toward home. For the young soldier to be on course for Miami, this needed to be the place they parted ways.

As he unloaded his backpack, Dozer leaped out of the car. Stephanie walked inside the motel lobby and asked if they accepted dogs. To her surprise, the desk clerk said, "Yes." Stephanie opened her purse and counted her cash. It totaled exactly $74.

"How much would it cost for one night?" she asked.

The clerk paused and did some figuring. Looking up, she said, "Well, ma'am, with tax and the extra fee for the dog, that will be seventy-four dollars." Sensing God's hand in this unlikely encounter, Stephanie immediately rented the room.

Stepping outside, she handed her new friend the key to a room where he could get a shower and a good night's sleep, assuring him that Dozer was welcome in the hotel too. He was surprised by this kind gesture, and saying their good-byes, both of them began to weep. After thanking her, he said, "Stephanie, please don't ever pick up a hitchhiker again. There are a lot of crazy people out there!" She promised to take his advice.

Pulling away from the curb, Stephanie realized God had sent a stranger and his dog to her on a night when she needed to be reminded that she was not alone and that God had a purpose and a plan for what he was doing in her life. The unexpected sloppy, wet kiss from Dozer and the encouraging companionship of his owner had brightened her drive home and given her a new perspective on this difficult season of her life.

That night she remembered something important. When

God seems the most absent, he is the most present—and he brings renewed joy to our hearts when we follow his lead.

> Why are you down in the dumps, dear soul? Why are you crying the blues? Fix my eyes on God— soon I'll be praising again. He puts a smile on my face. He's my God.
>
> —PSALM 43:5 MSG

Think optimistically about yourself and your
future. Give thanks to the One who has given
you everything, and trust in your heart that
he wants to give you so much more.[1]
—AUTHOR UNKNOWN

CHAPTER 34

Joy in the Ice Cream Parlor

BY JENNIE AFMAN DIMKOFF

"How's your writing coming, Jennie?" Shirley asked over the phone. "Got a story to share today? I loved the last one you told me about your parents selling their home. God really *is* in the miracle business, isn't he?"

Shirley is one of my most joyful friends. She also works for my brother-in-law, who is my agent for booking speaking engagements, and her cheerful voice and lilting laughter always bring a smile to my face.

I laughed. "Since you and your husband have been in ministry for years, I imagine *you* must know a wonderful 'God moment' story I should write for this book. Don't you have any great ideas for *me*?

Shirley was quiet for a moment and then replied, "I do know of a major miracle that God worked in my own life, Jennie." She hesitated and then went on. "It's not an easy story, but it's one that I've wanted to share for a long time."

"Okay. What would be a good title?"

She giggled. "Let's see. 'No More Prozac.' The subtitle could be 'The Antidepressant Gift'!"

"What?!" I choked.

"Just kidding. You'll think of a much better title than that," Shirley assured me.

Shirley had accepted the Lord at age nine and had been a good student and high achiever. When she grew older, she became a secretary. Anyone who knew her would have described her as confident, capable, and busy. Shirley was a perfectionist, and she felt it was her Christian duty to meet everyone's needs. She filled each slot in her planner, thinking that the good things she busied herself with made her a better person; conversely, she thought that saying no would bring God's disapproval.

She married a pastor and faced the heartbreak of infertility early in marriage, but she and Stan were blessed to adopt two children. God called them to a wonderful church and rewarding ministry, and while their children were young, Shirley worked at a series of part-time jobs, believing that her family's financial future depended upon her personal contribution.

"Jennie, it was during that time that a series of sad things happened," she told me. "My mother-in-law battled pancreatic cancer; my dad died unexpectedly; we dealt with one of our sons' rebellion and the divorce of the other, who had seen combat during the Gulf War. That was a pretty rough stretch, but with God's help, we managed to get through it."

With these events behind them, Shirley took a full-time position with a good salary and benefits. However, for the first time in her life, she found that no matter what she did, she seemed unable to satisfy the demands of management. It was a toxic environment, and the atmosphere was thick with both political correctness and deceit as employees jockeyed for positions of authority.

Shirley sighed deeply before going on. "In an attempt to please, I became a workaholic. Headaches and exhaustion kept me from many church activities, and as the pastor's wife, you can imagine how I struggled with guilt. It only added to my anxiety!"

"What happened then?" I asked.

"I began to experience panic attacks and wept uncontrollably. I had this feeling of sadness and hopelessness that never

went away. I became agoraphobic, which means I had unrea-
sonable fear and anxiety. It was horrible."

"How did your husband react to all of this?"

"Stan? Oh, he was worried sick and insisted that I take time
off."

Shirley went on to say that a two week vacation did nothing to help. When the thought of returning to work only
brought about a sense of dread, she phoned her boss and re-
signed before the following Monday.

Losing her job was the straw that broke the camel's back.
Shirley found herself in the throes of a major clinical depression. Seeking wise counsel, she learned to recognize the lies
she believed that had caused her to perform to the point of
exhaustion and destroyed her self-esteem. Instead, she learned
to turn to Scripture to discern the truth for herself. Months
passed, and Shirley was on the verge of living a normal life
again.

"Jennie, it *should* have been a day to celebrate . . . my last
counseling appointment! But instead I still felt frozen inside when I thought about the future. Then my counselor
said, 'Shirley, you have made excellent progress. You are now
equipped to handle whatever life brings, and you've worked
to develop your trust in the Lord. I don't believe we'll need to
set up any more appointments unless there is something we
haven't discussed that you'd like to talk about.'

"'But I'm afraid of trying to find a job!' I told him."

"It was my greatest fear, Jennie, and I just blurted it out."
Shirley continued. "I'd been off work for months, and trying to
find a job terrified me. I was sure employers would favor hiring
younger workers, and I worried about what they would think
regarding how abruptly I'd left my last position."

"Did the counselor offer good advice?" I asked.

Shirley chuckled over the phone. "He sure did! He reminded

me to write down the lie that the enemy was telling me and then tell him what God had to say about that in his Word. We covered that principle in our early sessions! However, I still felt insecure enough to schedule one last appointment."

As August advanced, Shirley had no job and no prospects, but she enjoyed a relaxing change of pace and often worked in her garden. Her time off also allowed her to spend time with her son when he returned home for a quick visit, nearing the end of his obligation to the army. He loved fishing, so the three of them enjoyed a day in a borrowed boat on a lake nearby. It was a wonderful, warm day, and at its conclusion they decided to stop by Baskin-Robbins to celebrate the end of summer. It was a decision that would change everything that Shirley had experienced in the last several months.

"We had just finished our ice cream when the door opened and a couple who looked vaguely familiar walked in. As we moved toward the exit they were scanning the menu, and in passing, my eyes met the woman's and she smiled at me warmly. Then, out of the corner of my eye I saw my husband shaking hands with her husband! It seemed they knew one another from Christian businessmen's luncheons, and the woman, Carol Kent, recognized me from our church and her years there as the teacher of an interdenominational Bible study! Our personal interaction had been brief, and I hadn't seen her in close to ten years. I was surprised that she even remembered me."

"You connected with my sister, Carol, at an ice cream store?" I asked in disbelief.

"Just listen to the rest." Shirley continued. "I'm telling you, Jennie, this is my *miracle* story!" She then explained to me that part of the amazing emotional healing that she had experienced was that she had been delivered from any shame regarding what she had endured earlier that year.

"Carol said, 'Tell me what you're doing these days, Shirley.'

"So I gave her my *Reader's Digest* version of the last several months . . . including the fact that I was recovering from clinical depression and that I was not currently working.

"Without a blink, Carol started telling me that she and Gene had just made a decision to begin a Christian speakers' agency and that they were hoping to add to their office staff . . . someone who could interact with both the public and the speakers to negotiate contracts and prepare them, as well as do other office work related to Carol's growing ministries.

"Then she asked if I'd be interested! They were going to be gone a few days on a ministry trip, but she said they would like to meet with me the following week when they were back! Without so much as looking in the want ads or filling out an application and without the need for that final appointment with my counselor, the Lord quite unexpectedly gave me the sweetest gift from heaven!"

I had a tear in my eye by this point in Shirley's story. I had no idea what her background had been. I just knew that she was a joy for the Kents to work with, and they were very thankful to have her on their staff.

"Shirley, do you have *any* idea how many times Carol and Gene have commented to me about how blessed they were the day you came to work for them?"

My friend was feeling a little emotional. "Jennie," she said, "aside from meeting Christ and my marriage, no other experience has ever proven to have such a long-lasting and positive influence in my life. Daily I'm given the opportunity to interact with others who are involved in ministry, to enjoy a stimulating and endless variety of activities, to meet members of the body of Christ from all across America, and to do so for the Kents, who regularly show their appreciation for my role on their ministry team with encouragement and generous praise.

I love Carol and Gene, and I will forever be grateful for how they have allowed the Lord to love me through this precious ministry. This job has truly been God's touch upon my life."

> May the God of hope fill you with all joy and peace
> as you trust in him, so that you may overflow with
> hope by the power of the Holy Spirit.
>
> —ROMANS 15:13 NIV

> It's not what you believe that counts. It's what you believe enough to do![1]
> —GARY GILBRANSON

CHAPTER 35

Saying Yes to God

BY CAROL KENT

Shannin was comfortable—in her relationships, her home, and her church. Coming from humble beginnings, she was quick to acknowledge gratefulness for her blessings—a loving husband, two delightful children, enough income to be generous, and multiple opportunities to serve in her church and in compassion-based organizations.

One weekend she and her husband opened their home for the annual youth retreat. That evening, the youth pastor showed a video depicting the plight of children in Uganda who were forced to leave their homes and sleep wherever they could hide to avoid being captured by rebel soldiers and forced to fight in a war that wasn't their own. As she watched, Shannin was overwhelmed with emotion. She could feel herself squirming inside.

Her thoughts swirled: *Is God speaking directly to me through this video?* Waves of emotion came over Shannin, and she longed to grab each of those sad-faced children and rescue them. She brushed away tears as the program ended and wondered if her desire to do something for those children would fade.

Over the next few days, instead of fading, her emotions grew more intense. Shannin fell to her knees and prayed. *Lord, what else do you want me to see? What else do I need to hear? I want my heart to break over the things that break your heart.*

• • •

Shannin's husband's job took him all over the globe. Soon after praying so intensely, she decided to be more than a tourist when she accompanied him on trips. Their next stop was Taiwan, and she had already researched which orphanage she would visit. After arriving, Shannin's heart was captured by a little girl who had been abandoned by her parents after her father threw her across the room, leaving her physically and mentally disabled. The caretakers in the orphanage were like mothers to the children, and Shannin observed the beautiful way they reached out to this child. She realized the loving atmosphere of an orphanage could be a supportive and meaningful home to abandoned children.

Arriving back in the United States, Shannin wrestled with her feelings. *Why do I have this strong desire to visit orphans? Is God asking us to adopt a child, or is this stirring in my soul something else?* She needed more information and supernatural wisdom.

The words poured out of her: *God, I don't want to miss the blessing you have for me and for my family, but I don't yet know what you want us to do. Please give me eyes that see and ears that hear your voice.*

Soon after she prayed, the phone rang. It was a friend telling her that she was going with a team of short-term missionaries to Honduras to build a medical clinic. Shannin and her husband decided to join the team and take their children, but they made plans to stay an extra week in order to visit a local orphanage. Arriving at the home, they were bombarded by numerous children who were starved for affection. Shannin felt great joy as she held the children, but she was simultaneously overcome with sadness. The child-care workers didn't even check to see who they were, and there was a total lack of supervision. One fifteen-year-old boy had become the father figure for the group, but he would be leaving soon due to his advanced age.

Shannin's compassion for orphans was deepening, and she often wept over the individual children she had already met and for those she might never meet. She and her family decided that they wanted to spend all of their future vacations visiting children in orphanages. Still, for Shannin, there were haunting questions: *How can I make lasting positive changes? Is adoption enough, or is God asking me to help more than one child?*

Soon after this prayer, Shannin had a renewed burden for the orphans of Africa. They were in a troubled part of the world, and she believed God was asking her to do something tangible to help. The Holy Spirit tugged at Shannin's heart, and as she prayed, she wept. *Lord, what if there are children who will suffer because I fail to obey you? Please show me what I am to do.*

Shannin was overwhelmed with love for needy children, including those she had never met, but who was *she* to dream of doing something big for kids on the other side of the world? What qualified her to be the person to organize help? Shannin's thoughts raced. *If not me, who? If not now, when?*

What happened next was a total surprise. Shannin met a man who was running an orphanage in the Democratic Republic of the Congo. He was a native of Africa but now lived in her hometown of Lakeland, Florida. He was planning to finish building an orphanage in Africa. After weeks of meetings and a commitment to get personally involved, Shannin and her family were on a plane headed to Africa.

The needs there were beyond anything Shannin had witnessed before. It was a "survival of the fittest" environment. Children found their way to the orphanage due to war, disease, or abandonment. Parents lacking the resources to care for their weak and sickly children discarded them. The caregivers did not "waste" their time on nurturing the young residents, and they never displayed affection. They commented on how strange it was that these visitors from the United States liked to hold the children.

During this time Shannin saw listless and lethargic children respond so powerfully to human touch and genuine love that they danced in the river during bath time. Most of the children did not know their birth dates. Some had no name. Many did not remember how they got to the orphanage. Over the next two years, Shannin's entire family got involved in fund-raising and donating money to the orphans of Africa, but once again, there was a tug in her heart and she began to pray for God to reveal his next step to her.

As Shannin prayed and read God's word, she kept a journal: *Lord, give me eyes to see your plan. I feel your prompting in my heart again. I have a restlessness that makes me eager to see and to do what you have on my agenda next.*

A few days later, a friend called and told Shannin she wanted to introduce her to a woman who had a heart for orphans much like she did. A meeting was scheduled for the next week. Shannin's children accompanied her, and when they arrived, Shannin's friend Kaylene introduced them to the guest of honor.

The woman began to speak, and within seconds, Shannin knew she was sitting in the middle of a divine appointment. The woman spoke of property she owned in Tanzania, a country situated on the eastern side of Africa. She wanted to have an orphanage built there. Speaking slowly, she said, "I am seventy-eight years old. I have the vision of what needs to be done, but I am exhausted. I cannot do it alone. I would like to give you the property so you can build an orphanage and care for the children in this needy part of the continent you already care so much about."

In that moment, Shannin saw clearly the vision she had

prayed for. She had put some money aside, and she instantly knew God wanted the funds to go toward building the orphanage on the property in Tanzania. She thanked the remarkable woman as she accepted the property and the weighty responsibility that came with it.

Shannin's daughter Corrine was sitting in the passenger seat next to her mom. There were tears in her eyes. She, too, had been deeply impacted by this unexpected encounter. Suddenly, she looked up and said, "Mom, I don't want to be lukewarm as a Christian. I've been reading about what the Bible says about this. For some people a once-a-year missions trip is a big deal, if that is what God wants them to do; but for me, if we don't build this orphanage in Tanzania, I'd be lukewarm. I know God wants us to move forward! We *have* to do it!"

God had touched Shannin and her daughter simultaneously—the work was not too big for them to accomplish and he would supply everything that was needed as they said yes, to him.*

But you have God-blessed eyes—eyes that see! And God-blessed ears—ears that hear!

—MATTHEW 13:16 MSG

----

* Shannin Pickle is the president of Small Steps for Compassion with the Make it Count Foundation. They are currently raising funds to build an orphanage in Tanzania. To find out how you can help, go to www.themakeit countfoundation.com.

I once scorned ev'ry fearful thought of death
When it was but the end of pulse and breath
But now my eyes have seen that past the pain
There is a world that's waiting to be claimed.[1]

—CALVIN MILLER

CHAPTER 36

Homeward Bound

BY JENNIE AFMAN DIMKOFF

Forty-one-year-old Steve Campbell had never let his failing health stand in the way of his encouraging others and living life as fully as possible. After his first stroke at thirty-six, there had been many emergency trips to the hospital, including three episodes of cardiac arrest where the feverish work of the medical staff had brought him back again and again. In fact, Steve had technically died so many times that people would ask him what it was like. He'd laugh and say, "I must have had a brain cramp, because I don't remember a thing!"

On the morning of his final collapse, he had breakfast with a man simply to encourage him. Then he had gone home and paid all the bills (each week he made sure that everything was in order, just in case), and then he had gone to lunch with a friend. He collapsed at the restaurant. In the small town of Nappanee, Indiana, it wasn't unusual that others at the restaurant knew Steve. A nurse friend was there having lunch, and when he crumpled to the floor, she performed CPR. He was rushed to the hospital about thirty minutes away.

Steve was diagnosed with congestive heart failure, and his health was so critical that hospital officials didn't think his wife, Adelle, would arrive in time, but she did, as did their two teenagers, who arrived much later. In fact, God graciously allowed Steve five days to say good-bye. Between labored breaths, he gave thirty-seven-year-old Adelle and his children, fifteen-year-old Caleb and thirteen-year-old Melissa, words of farewell they would cherish.

Steve told his kids that his only sadness in dying was that his time with them would be cut short. He thanked Adelle with a wink and a chuckle for keeping his life so "abnormally" full. She was a nurse, but in spite of his illness, he had always urged her to accept speaking engagements around the country to share her own remarkable story. He had been her greatest cheerleader and had wanted her to be independent and confident enough to be able to go on without him when the time came.

Each day found him gasping for breath yet so concerned about the feelings of others as they came in to visit. Wracked with pain, he somehow managed to keep his sense of humor to the end, and Steve cheered others up who had intended to bring him encouragement.

During those five precious days, he reviewed with Adelle his perpetual list of things she was to do when he died. First, call to make the funeral arrangements. Then take care of the business and household expenses that he had always taken care of. He wanted to make sure she remembered everything. She would have to take care of everything now.

"Just rest, and you'll feel better soon," Adelle whispered on that last day.

"Not this time, sweetheart," he whispered with a tired smile.

In the end, he pulled out his own breathing tube, not wanting to be sustained. Adelle was right there with him. He wanted to sit up in the reclining chair beside the bed, feeling that he would be able to breathe a bit easier in that position and perhaps sleep a bit, so Adelle helped him. She lay on his bed right beside him, very aware of his labored breathing, and she may have dozed, because at five AM she was startled when all the medical equipment started going off.

Leaping from the bed, Adelle knelt on the floor in front of the chair and took Steve's left hand in both of hers and just held it. He opened his eyes and used the last of his strength to move his right hand to rest over hers, and looking down at her, he said, "I love you." His eyes closed, and he slipped from this life to be with his Lord.

Adelle knelt there, savoring that sweet good-bye, and after a few moments, she stood, bent over her husband, and kissed his forehead. There was no panic in that small room. Steve and Adelle had understood that with the seriousness of Steve's condition, any day might be his last. They chose to live life with no regrets, they had made precious memories, and they had savored each day, understanding that the good-bye was coming. They were grateful God had allowed it to be gentle.

The time of death was recorded at five fifteen AM. Nurses came and quietly moved Steve's body to the bed. The medical equipment was strangely silent, the screens dark. Then precious friends came and gathered around the bed, and the room was silent no longer. Instead it was filled with the sweet strains of "Amazing Grace, how sweet the sound . . ." and reverent, heartfelt words of praise from the Doxology: *Praise God from whom all blessings flow. Praise him all creatures here below. Praise him above ye heavenly host. Praise Father, Son, and Holy Ghost. Amen.*

You are blessed when you feel you have lost what is most dear to you. Only then can you be embraced by the One most dear to you.

—MATTHEW 5:4 MSG

> God will not permit any troubles to come upon
> us, unless He has a specific plan by which great
> blessing can come out of the difficulty.[1]
>
> —PETER MARSHALL

CHAPTER 37

The Night That Changed Everything

BY CAROL KENT

It was Christmas Eve. Suzanne, now in her sophomore year of college, was home for the holidays. Before she left for school in September of 1960, she and her boyfriend had broken up. Throughout the fall months they had not written, called, or contacted each other. They had been high school sweethearts, but both realized the romance was completely over.

For the past several years their families had celebrated the night before Christmas at the home of friends—and this year was no different. The adults had their party downstairs, and the college crowd congregated upstairs. The upperclassmen put together a drink called a "scorpion," which was a combination of liquors they served in a beautiful sterling silver punch bowl. A straw was placed in the bowl, and it was passed from person to person. Suzanne's friends coaxed her to participate and she played along. With her limited experience with alcohol, the drink tasted like strong punch. Suzanne assumed everyone was drinking from the bowl just like she was, not realizing the group was goading her into a drunken state while they barely sipped the beverage. Before long she was intoxicated and struggling to stand up without assistance.

Moments later her former boyfriend stopped by the house to wish everyone a merry Christmas. When he entered the room, the instigators of this perverse entertainment were relieved. They explained what had happened and asked him to drive her home. He happily obliged and carefully took her down the back steps, so the adults on the first floor wouldn't discover what had happened.

In retrospect, no one should have been more surprised by what took place than Dave. They hadn't drunk alcohol during the entire time they'd dated. That night, instead of taking Suzanne home, he took her to his apartment. She had never been in his apartment before, because she wanted to avoid the appearance of impropriety. During their months of dating, Suzanne and Dave had shown great affection for each other, but they had never slept together. Throughout their earlier dating relationship they had made an agreement that they would never go that far before marriage.

Despite her drunken state, Suzanne remembers being happy to see Dave walk through the door. She realized her need to leave and willingly got into his car, assuming he was taking her home. Instead, he took her to his apartment, but she was too intoxicated to know where she was.

Once they arrived, Suzanne was unable to walk without assistance, and Dave guided her inside and laid her down on his bed. He told her she needed to eat something and went to the kitchen in search of food. Moments later she passed out. As Suzanne lay unconscious on his bed, Dave took advantage of her sexually. On Christmas Eve of 1960, Suzanne was date-raped by her former boyfriend.

With guilt closing in after the attack, Dave grabbed her by the shoulders and started shaking Suzanne frantically as he yelled, "Wake up! Wake up! I've gone too far!" Slowly, Suzanne awakened and strained to understand what had taken place.

The first week in January, heartsick and ridden with false guilt over what had happened, Suzanne headed back to college. She never planned to be in contact with Dave again. A few weeks passed, and when she was late for her period, panic set in. During the last week of the month, she drove home and made an appointment with Dr. Charles, a gynecologist and family friend. A test confirmed her worst fear—she was pregnant.

Suzanne's mind raced. Returning to college and over-whelmed with fear, she contemplated suicide. Her father was a politician, and their family was well-known in their community and far beyond. With great angst she thought about the public embarrassment and shame her pregnancy would bring to the family.

She soon realized she lacked the courage to take her own life, so Suzanne called Dave, the former boyfriend she never planned to see again, and told him she was pregnant. He immediately picked her up at school and drove her to her parents' home. Her mom and dad were shocked and in emotional turmoil following this unexpected news. They took Suzanne to meet with a couple in another city fifty miles away where they had arranged for this pastor and his wife to adopt her baby. Suzanne was in a daze, but when she fully understood the purpose of the meeting, she spoke up. "I don't think you understand. My baby is *not* going to be put up for adoption. I am going to give birth to this baby and raise it myself!"

Her father pointed to the exit and forcefully replied, "Do you see that door over there? You have two choices—you can either walk through that door and never look back or you can marry Dave!" When Suzanne wouldn't agree to adoption, her mother and father planned her private wedding. With only her immediate family in attendance, Suzanne's rushed marriage quietly took place out of town just two days later on February 4, 1961.

Suzanne knew she had shattered her parents' rosy dream for her life and didn't want to cause them more distress. The marriage was a struggle, but Suzanne desperately wanted to make up for their complicated and difficult beginning, and she longed for a good life for her child. Jimmy was born on September 11, 1961, and five years later she delivered a second son on June 15, 1966. Dave had gone fishing and wasn't there during her labor and delivery. For five and a half years she tried to make the marriage work. In his own way, Dave tried, too, but they were young and both were haunted by the circumstances that led to their marriage. There was more than enough guilt to go around, and she and Dave eventually divorced.

Life was challenging and Suzanne struggled on multiple levels. When Jimmy was young, she wrote to Ann Landers and asked her how and when she should tell her son about his conception. Ann wrote back and said, "You will know *how* and *when* at the right time. Good luck, dear!"

• • •

Twenty years passed. Jimmy was finishing his freshman year at Stanford University, and he had returned home on the eve of Suzanne's fortieth birthday. As Suzanne and Jimmy sat up talking late into the night, she instinctively knew it was time to tell him the truth and she shared the entire story with her son. It was as if God had already prepared his heart for this unexpected news.

The next day Jimmy pulled out the gift he had wrapped for her birthday. It was a Bible. He said, "Mom, one month ago I invited Jesus Christ into my life." He spoke at length about what it meant to become a Christian. He explained, "God has a purpose and a plan, and it was no accident I was conceived under such unusual circumstances."

Suzanne explained, "That day my son introduced me to a personal relationship with Jesus Christ. He had come to faith at the university where he was finishing up his first year. He gave me a beautiful Bible and wrote a letter to accompany the gift."

Dear Mom,

    I cannot imagine anything in the world that I would rather give you on your birthday than the word of God. The fact that every scripture found in it is inspired by God, provides the basis for our faith. . . . When used with the guidance of the Holy Spirit, it will enable you to grow in your knowledge of the Lord. . . . I believe you will find that trusting in Him is the greatest comfort imaginable . . .

    I love you with all my heart, and wish you a beautiful fortieth birthday. God bless you always, and may he bring out even more of the infinite potential that exists inside your loving heart . . .

Love,

Jimmy

Now, twenty-nine years later, Suzanne and Jimmy welcome opportunities to talk to each other about how God is at work in their lives. They honestly share the circumstances of Jimmy's conception with others and agree that if only one woman is encouraged to carry a baby to full term and not seek abortion as a solution to an unwanted pregnancy, it is worth their decision to be open about their journey.

God's gift to Suzanne came through adversity and revealed his sovereignty. The date rape that resulted in an unwanted pregnancy produced a beloved son who introduced her to Christ and as a pastor during the past twenty-four years, he has also introduced Christ to countless others.

God makes everything come out right; he puts victims back on their feet.

—PSALM 103:6 MSG

Thank you, Lord, for this bright day that
I have spent just talking with a friend. For
on our meeting, you were there.[1]
—MARION STROUD

CHAPTER 38

Going Back

BY JENNIE AFMAN DIMKOFF

I was lost in thought as my husband, Graydon, walked in the door and kissed me on the cheek. "What came in the mail?" he asked.

Jerking back to the present, I lifted up the paper I held in my hand. "An invitation to my class reunion—*forty years!*" I said in disbelief. "*Old* people have fortieth reunions. This is depressing!"

He laughed. "No, it isn't. I took my ninety-two-year-old mother to her reunion last year, and only two people from her class showed up." He grinned widely. "You, my sweet, are still a spring chicken!"

I laughed. "If you're trying to make me feel younger, it's not working!"

"Do you want to go?" he asked. "I'll go with you."

"Maybe. The date is open on our calendar. I'll let you know. Okay?"

Did I want to go back? I had only lived in Sandusky, Michigan, for three and a half years, so other than that short time, I didn't have much history there. My dad was a pastor, and since he had been called to another church the year after I graduated, every break found us visiting either Graydon's parents or my parents in their respective communities rather than going back to my high school alma mater. I had been back only once in forty years.

I had some wonderful memories. The high school plays and musicals had been highlights for me, and there were a few friends I still kept in touch with at Christmastime. But there were painful memories too. I had been a class officer and a leader, and I tried to assume those roles with enthusiasm and grace. However, as I grew older, I realized that constantly getting leading roles in the school plays and musicals must have irked some. The old adage "Kids can be cruel" was oh so true, and I experienced it firsthand. By the time I graduated, I was ready to move on to college. Did I *really* want to go back?

Over the next several days my mind was flooded with memories from the past, some lovely, others not. I had started babysitting for neighbors at age twelve and from then on had assumed responsibility for buying all my own clothing. I earned fifty cents an hour, so it took quite a while to earn enough to buy even one item.

I had seven outfits that I rotated for school. After all these years, I still have the vivid memory of finally saving up enough money to purchase a two-piece outfit in a local department store that had been advertised in *Seventeen* magazine. It was a perfect fit, and I loved the navy top with the knit collar that matched the cute, multicolored corduroy skirt. I remember taping the picture from the magazine on the mirror in my bedroom. I finally had an eighth outfit to add to the rotation, and it wasn't homemade! I could hardly wait to wear it to school.

I felt like a model that Monday morning. It was amazing what those new clothes did for my self-esteem. However, in the midafternoon I grabbed a hall pass to use the restroom and was shocked to hear a voice behind me in the hallway call, "If you realized what a clown you look like in that skirt, you'd never wear it again!"

I jerked around to see who my attacker was and tried to laugh as if I were reacting to a joke, but tears of humiliation blurred my vision and I turned and rushed to the restroom. I locked myself in a stall and wept. In my immaturity, I *believed* the vicious words that had been so carelessly flung in my direction, and even though I had worked very hard to afford that beautiful outfit, I didn't wear it again for over two months.

Did I *want* to go back to a place where multiple memories of good times and mean girls intertwined? Forty years later as I was reliving old memories, it occurred to me it was likely that the girl who so flippantly said those words probably didn't even remember the incident. How odd it was that I remembered her words and the pain they caused so vividly, but I could no longer recall her name or her face. Suddenly, I was smiling, and I bowed my head and prayed.

Lord, thank you for healing old wounds. I remember reading somewhere that when you help us to forgive others, you won't give us a case of "holy amnesia" but that you will drain the pain from our wounds. I realize today that you did that for me a long time ago with that classmate. Father, if I go back to my reunion, will you help me to represent you well? I don't want to go back nursing old wounds or trying to look like a celebrity. My classmates do not need to see me as a platform person or a speaker or author. I'd like them to see you. In Jesus' name, amen.

That afternoon I was visiting with my neighbor in the backyard and mentioned I had finally decided to go back to my class reunion.

"I never go to my reunions," he said. "It's always the same old cliques that sit together and exclude people. After going to two of them, I've never bothered going again."

I smiled. "Well, Graydon will be with me, so I won't be totally alone. There are a few people I'd really like to see, and after that, I've decided I'm going to circulate and look for people in the room who seem lonely and make them feel welcome!"

As the reunion approached I was a little nervous about what to wear but excited to see old friends and renew acquaintances. When we arrived, the name tags had our original senior pictures printed beside our names, which was helpful for identifying people. After forty years, hair had changed, receded, or disappeared, and several waistlines had expanded.

We were immediately surrounded by welcoming classmates, and conversation flowed easily. Rather than the competitive one-upmanship I remembered from the past, there was genuine interest and friendliness. Time, life experiences, success, and disappointments had both enriched lives and taken their toll. I had the pleasant thought that maturity mellows people and they are more gracious to one another as a result.

As the evening progressed I remembered my pledge to look for lonely people, so I excused myself from our table, only to have a lovely woman seek *me* out. My eyes immediately went to her name tag, but there was no accompanying photo. Her name was Vicki.

"Jennie," she said, "you wouldn't remember me, but I was so hoping you would be here tonight. Would it be possible for me to speak to you privately at some point this evening?"

I assured her that I was available at that moment, and we stepped into a little courtyard outside the restaurant.

"I was two years younger than you in school, Jennie, but I remember you and your sister Paula, who was in my class," Vicki told me. "I lived a wild and crazy life back then—and I made some poor choices that I'm not proud of. But I want you to know that I watched you and your sister, and I admired you from afar. You made a big impression on me, even though you never knew it."

She went on to say that life hadn't been easy for her, but five years before, she had come to know Jesus Christ as her personal savior and soon thereafter her husband had also become a Christian.

"Everything about our lives has changed, Jennie," she said with her face shining. "We still have some challenges with our boys, but there is true joy and peace in our lives now in the place of despair."

"Oh, Vicki," I responded, "you have no idea how much it means to me that you've shared this news with me tonight. I almost didn't come, and I would have missed hearing your story. It has turned out to be the highlight of my whole evening!"

"It has?" she asked. "I want to tell you something else, Jennie. Back in high school, I thought that your family must be perfect and that you never had to deal with pain or heartache like other people. Well, I went to a conference this spring with some ladies from my church and heard your sister Carol speak. She told about the heartache in her family, but through it all she gave honor to the Lord. I realized as I was listening that no one is immune to suffering, but we can choose to react to it in far different ways. I learned so much from her talk. Please tell her that."

"I will do that. We're working on a new book together called *Miracle on Hope Hill,* so I'll be in touch with her soon. May I pray with you, Vicki? I'd like to thank God for this special reunion and pray for you and your husband and your boys."

Tears came to Vicki's eyes. "You would do that?"

"I'd like to very much."

Placing an arm around my new friend's shoulders I thanked the Lord for the opportunity to look back once in a while and be reminded of all that God has done in our lives. I prayed for Vicki's family concerns, and together we returned to the reunion. My heart was singing, and later I privately thanked my heavenly father for the gift of the sweet class reunion blessing he had given us both that night.

You always remember us kindly and long to see us,
as we long to see you.

—I THESSALONIANS 3:6 ESV

We make a living by what we get; we
make a life by what we give.[1]
—SIR WINSTON CHURCHILL

CHAPTER 39

Chocolate-Covered Cherries

BY CAROL KENT

Gene pulled the receiver away from his ear and simply said, "My dad's gone. He went to sleep peacefully last night and never woke up. The memorial service will be this Saturday. I didn't even get to say good-bye."

Just six weeks earlier Dad had flown from Michigan to Florida for a break from the winter snow and to spend some family time with us. He was eighty-two years old and suffered from multiple health challenges, so we were thrilled he could make the trip. Dad hadn't been on a plane since he was in the army during his early twenties and he had so much fun seeing the earth from a bird's-eye view.

The next two weeks were filled with activities. The Webster Flea Market came first—one square mile of booths displaying every imaginable type of clothing, crafts, leather goods, lawn ornaments, and jewelry, both new and used, and at drastically reduced prices. Dad carefully selected items he knew his grandchildren would enjoy as gifts. Then came the trip to the Strawberry Festival in Plant City. We gorged ourselves on the biggest strawberry shortcakes on the menu, complete with mounds of vanilla ice cream and topped off with whipped cream. Dad was living in the moment, engaging the waitresses in conversation and teasing the children around him in a playful, lighthearted manner. In retrospect, I think he knew that his health was declining and life was a gift that should not be wasted or taken lightly.

Over the course of his two-week visit, we noticed that whenever Dad left the house, he always came back with candy. He had a weakness for chocolate-covered cherries—he could down an entire one-pound box in a single sitting. Sometimes he tried to hide his cache inside a shopping bag or a newspaper, and when he thought we weren't looking, he popped a treat from his stash into his mouth. His eyes twinkled—just like those of a mischievous kid who had a secret.

Our favorite times were family dinners. Dad enjoyed talking about his past experiences working on the railroad, but he also had a new passion. He and his wife had begun volunteering their time at an inner-city kitchen that provided meals for the homeless. It was the joy of his life—helping people who were down and out.

Several days into the visit Dad went to a Christian bookstore and picked up a couple of sing-along DVDs of great hymns. He had acute hearing loss and I found myself cringing when he turned the volume up way past my comfort level. Moments later I heard a surprising sound. It was Dad singing off-key, right along with the video. The song was about heaven. His eyes were closed and a slight smile curved its way around the corners of his mouth. I knew Dad was thinking about a glorious place he was headed for soon. The volume no longer annoyed me, and I treasured the beauty of the moment.

• • •

Dad's memorial service was on Easter weekend. During the following few weeks, I noticed my husband's usual upbeat disposition had turned melancholy. One day I walked into his office and saw a half-empty box of chocolate-covered cherries on his desk. He had obviously downed several of the candies before I caught him.

"Gene," I exclaimed, "you don't even *like* chocolate-covered cherries. What's going on?"

He said, "Last week I was going through an old pile of Christmas cards I found in my desk drawer. The card from my dad had a thirty-dollar Wal-Mart gift card enclosed, and I suddenly realized it's the last gift I'll ever get from my father. I know I need to spend this on something special in his honor and I thought the decision would come more easily over a box of chocolate-covered cherries. I think I know what to do. Are you free to come with me to the store?"

We got in the car and drove to Wal-Mart. Gene's face reflected a total change in demeanor. He was exuberant as he grabbed a cart and headed toward the grocery section of the superstore. I had to walk quickly to keep up with him. He began gathering canned goods off the shelves—a wide variety of soups, different kinds of vegetables, fruit juices, five cans of Spam, and two tins of sardines. "We ate a lot of Spam when I was growing up, and my dad loved sardines too," he said. On the way to the checkout counter, Gene grabbed a one-pound box of chocolate-covered cherries and added it to this unusual cart of groceries.

With a smile on his face, he got out the treasured gift card and handed it to the clerk, along with some cash from his wallet. I was still a bit mystified as we loaded the sacks of food into our car. Gene headed downtown and parked in front of our local food pantry. He disappeared inside with the bags, but I noticed he left the box of candy on the front seat. I smiled as I began to understand the joy my husband was experiencing as he honored his father's memory by donating food to the homeless and disadvantaged people in our community.

When Gene returned, he opened the car door, pulled me

out of the front seat with one hand, and grabbed the choco-late-covered cherries with the other. "Let's grab a cup of coffee at the café on the corner and remember Dad's life. He loved to help needy people, and his example of being generous to oth-ers is the most powerful way he impacted my life."

That afternoon we sipped coffee and ate chocolate-covered cherries as we discussed the highlights of a life well lived by serving others.

I thank my God every time I remember you.

—PHILIPPIANS 1:3, NIV

ACKNOWLEDGMENTS

Miracle on Hope Hill was inspired by growing up hearing the stories our mother told us from our earliest days and by observing her dramatic vocal inflection as her stories unfolded. We listened with bated breath, wondering how the plots would thicken or what would happen to our favorite characters in the end. Due to Mama's influence, we began telling stories long before we knew we would both grow up to be public speakers and authors. We know it was our dear mother, Pauline Afman, who passed on the art of storytelling to us, and we are grateful.

No book like this could have been written without the involvement of many people who shared their personal journeys with us and granted permission to share their encounters with God's remarkable touch on their lives at unexpected moments. The miracle stories in this book are all true experiences of ordinary people who discovered hope in the middle of challenging or unusual situations. We are grateful for the generous contributions of all those who participated in this project.

A big shout-out goes to Cindy Lambert for catching the vision for this book and to John and Chrys Howard for appreciating the heartfelt quality of the stories and recognizing their potential to touch the hearts of others. We are also thankful to Philis Boultinghouse and Jessica Wong for their excellent editorial direction. Thanks, too, to Howard Books for making it possible for these stories to be in print. Most of all, we are grateful to you, our readers, for giving wings to this book by sharing these stories with others.

NOTES

CHAPTER 1

1. www.thinkexist.com.

CHAPTER 2

1. http://enrichmentjournal.ag.org/top/fruit5_kindness.cfm.

CHAPTER 3

1. William Ward, quoted in Lloyd Cory, *Quotable Quotations* (Wheaton, IL: Victor Books, 1985), 186.

CHAPTER 4

1. Percy Bysshe Shelley, www. brainyquote.com.

CHAPTER 5

1. www.brainyquote.com/quotes/quotes/m/masoncoole395061.html.

CHAPTER 6

1. Kathy Troccoli, quoted in Family Christian Stores, *100 Days of Praise for Women* (Grand Rapids, MI: Family Christian Stores, 2008), 126.

CHAPTER 7

1. Dee Brestin, *The God of All Comfort* (Grand Rapids, MI: Zondervan, 2009), 189.

CHAPTER 8

1. www.sermoncentral.com.

CHAPTER 9

1. C. Neil Strait, quoted in Cory, *Quotable Quotations,* 295.

CHAPTER 10

1. Barbara Johnson, quoted in Family Christian Stores, *100 Days of Praise for Women,* 111.

CHAPTER 11

1. V. Raymond Edman, quoted in Cory, *Quotable Quotations,* 130.

CHAPTER 12

1. Marion Stroud, *Dear God, It's Me and It's Urgent* (Grand Rapids: Discover House Publishers, 2008, 1.

CHAPTER 13

1. Rick Warren, *The Purpose Driven Life* (Grand Rapids, MI: Zondervan, 2002), 63.

CHAPTER 14

1. Abraham Lincoln, quoted in Gordon S. Jackson, *Quotes for the Journey* (Colorado Springs: NavPress, 2000), 124.
2. Jay Walsh, *Against All Odds* (Harrisburg: ABWE, 1996), 116–17.
3. Viggo B. Olson, *Daktar: Diplomat in Bangladesh* (Chicago: Moody Press, 1973), 266.

CHAPTER 15

1. www.mutahed.com/7.aspx.

CHAPTER 16

1. Gloria Gaither, quoted in Family Christian Stores, *100 Days of Praise for Women,* 126.

CHAPTER 17

1. Kay Arthur, quoted in Judith Couchman, *One Holy Passion* (Colorado Springs, CO: Waterbrook Press, 1998), 95.
2. Philippians 3:10 NIV.
3. I Peter 2:23 NLT.

CHAPTER 19

1. William Arthur Ward, quoted in Billy and Janice Hughey, *A Rainbow of Hope* (Rainbow Studios, Inc., 1994), 72.

CHAPTER 20

1. Nicole Johnson, quoted in Mary Ann Froehlich, *Living with Thorns* (Grand Rapids: Discovery House Publishers, 2009), 51.

CHAPTER 21

1. www.bellaonline.com.

CHAPTER 23

1. Jan Johnson, *Living a Purpose-Full Life* (Colorado Springs, CO: Waterbrook Press, 1999), 16.

CHAPTER 24

1. Emilie Barnes, quoted in Family Christian Stores, *100 Days of Praise for Women*, 126.

CHAPTER 25

1. Brenda Waggoner, *The Velveteen Woman* (Colorado Springs, CO: Chariot Victor Publishing, 1999), 88, 149.
2. Sarah Young, *Jesus Calling* (Nashville, TN: Thomas Nelson, 2004), 199.

CHAPTER 26

1. Abraham Lincoln, quoted in Michelle Cox and John Perrodin, *Simple Little Words* (Colorado Springs: Honor Books, 2008), 172.

CHAPTER 27

1. Corrie ten Boom, *Clippings from My Notebook* (Minneapolis, MN: World Wide Publications, 1982), 27.

CHAPTER 28

1. Oswald Chambers, quoted in Cox and Perrodin, *Simple Little Words*, 54.

CHAPTER 29

1. www.thinkexist.com.

CHAPTER 30

1. Sarah Young, *Jesus Lives* (Nashville, TN: Thomas Nelson, 2009), 170.

CHAPTER 31

1. Sam J. Ervin Jr., quoted in Albert M. Wells Jr., *Inspiring Quotations* (Nashville, TN: Thomas Nelson Publishers, 1988), 67.
2. Luke 1:38b KJV.

CHAPTER 32

1. Barbara Johnson, quoted in Family Christian Stores, *100 Days of Praise for Women,* 67.

CHAPTER 33

1. http://dailychristianquote.com/dcqcomfort2.html.

CHAPTER 34

1. Family Christian Stores, *100 Days of Praise for Women,* 313.

CHAPTER 35

1. Gary Gilbranson, quoted in Richard Stearns, *The Hole in Our Gospel* (Nashville, TN: World Vision, Inc., 2009), 87.

CHAPTER 36

1. Calvin Miller, quoted in Randy Alcorn, *Heaven* (Carol Stream, IL: Tyndale House Publishers, Inc., 2004), 3.

CHAPTER 37

1. www.motivational-inspirational-corner.com.

CHAPTER 38

1. Stroud, *Dear God, It's Me and It's Urgent,* 176.

CHAPTER 39

1. www.quotationspage.com/quote/2236.html.

Printed in the United States
By Bookmasters